AN
ORPHAN'S
TALE

Mardiros Manuelian, Providence, Rhode Island, circa 1930

AN ORPHAN'S TALE

AN ACCOUNT OF WHY I LEFT HOME
AND WHAT HAPPENED AFTERWARDS

MARDIROS MANUELIAN

EDITED BY PETER MANUELIAN

Aratsani Press

An Orphan's Tale: An Account of Why I Left Home and What Happened Afterwards
© 2016 by Peter M. Manuelian

All rights reserved.
Published in the United States by Aratsani Press.

No part of this book may be reproduced in any manner whatsoever without prior written permission of the author, except in the case of brief quotations embodied in critical articles or reviews.

Unless otherwise noted, all photos (cover and interiors) are © the Manuelian family

Book and Cover design: Vladimir Verano, Third Place Press

ARATSANI PRESS
2752 Northeast 97th Street
Seattle, WA 98115

Author contact: pmanuelian@gmail.com

ISBN: 978-0-692-59778-1

To all those who have been uprooted from their native lands

TABLE OF CONTENTS

Introduction	i
My Village	1
Family Life	5
Genocide	8
Living with the Turks – at Tar Agha's	14
Flight to Kharpert	22
In the Kharpert Orphanage	26
Leaving the Kharpert Orphanage and Turkey	32
Syria and Lebanon	38
To Constantinople by Sea	40
From Constantinople to Greece	44
Corfu	45
After the Orphanage: Macedonia and Thrace	50
Back to Athens	60
On to Marseille, France, by Sea	64
To Paris and Canada	67
Photos	70
Canada	76
In The United States: Providence, Rhode Island	82
New York City	88
Married and Living in New York	92
Editor's End Notes	95

INTRODUCTION

In the early 1950s my father wrote an account of his life. He hand-wrote in English, which he was familiar with but not proficient in, and filled up four lined 8 ½ x 11 inch pads. I suspect he did not write in Armenian, a language in which he was more comfortable, because he wanted an English-reading audience to know about what he had experienced. The account begins with a bit of background to his village life, but he starts to record actual events when he is a child of about eight during the Armenian genocide of 1915. He then describes what he went through and endured as he was growing up, and takes it up to 1950 when he has a family and is an established small businessman in New York City.

Over 20 years later he showed me what he had written and entrusted the writing pads to me, his son. At the time I was too engrossed with the events of my own young life to pay much attention to his. I read his account and put it aside. I jotted down questions I had about what had occurred and now and then over the years would ask him to expand on particular incidents. The last discussions we had about the events of his early life took place during the year prior to his death in October 2002 at the age of 95.

Later I discovered three other pieces of writing of from four to seven pages, each one composed in the 1980s. They all begin from the beginning, as though he were still trying to come to terms with and exorcise the trauma of his childhood experiences. He focuses on these events of 1915 and shortly thereafter and not as much on his life after he left Turkey. In each of these later pieces he repeats such phrases as, "My grandfather was taken away by the police and never heard from," or "When he left he said he was going to the city to bring me candy; I'm still waiting for that candy 70 years later." Or, "My mother and sisters were taken away, did not know what happened to them," or "Women and girls, raped and tortured and killed for the kick of it," or "I was 8 years old, half-starved most of the time, in rags all of the time, in cold winter and hot summer, suffering and sick urchin no one cares for." He ends the piece written last with, "Lost everything during my childhood, all my kin, and my youth. Thank god I was alive." While several of his relatives did survive, as this account relates, nonetheless the experience of being wrenched from his home and family at the age of eight must have been so traumatic for the young boy that he saw it as a total loss.

Until the end he had a lucid mind. During the first few days of October 2001 when I was in New York City for my mother's funeral I asked him what he thought had happened on September 11th. Without pause, he said, "The Turks attacked us." Of course, he knew that it hadn't literally been the Turks, but he conflated such a horrific event as 9/11 with his own experience more than 85 years before and he used "Turks" as a catchall description of those who would commit such violent acts. The loss he felt stayed with him throughout his life, although it did not prevent him from enjoying life and moving ahead as best as he could. He was, in the best sense of the word, a survivor, one who would shrug off adversity by considering that it could have been worse.

The following account, then, is based on his writings in the 1950s, with some details added from conversations over 30 years. I have revised the syntax and grammar, particularly the verb tenses, and have corrected the spelling to make it more readable, but I have retained his phrasing. While all of the language here does not appear in my father's original, all of the descriptions of events, and his responses to them, are his. Words in brackets are the editor's; words in parentheses, the author's.

He did not give a title to his account. I chose *An Orphan's Tale* because he frequently uses the words "orphan" or "orphanage" and presents his life experiences in a straightforward chronological story. I have also added a table of contents and explanatory end notes.

Now, 100 years after the tragic 1915 genocide of the Armenians in their homeland tore him from his life up to then, Mardiros Manuelian's short account of his early life is being published. We can follow him as he moves from being a child orphaned in 1915, experiencing the wrenching loss of his family, to an adult in another world, creating his own family. It is a tale spanning three continents and covering almost 50 years. I hope you will find it interesting, informative, and touching.

Peter Manuelian
December 2015
Seattle, Washington

AN

ORPHAN'S

TALE

MY VILLAGE

I was born during the winter of 1907 in Segham, one of the many Armenian villages on the outskirts of Palu, a provincial market town, in the eastern Ottoman Empire. Palu, sometimes spelled Paloo, or Palou, on old maps, is a small city on the left bank of a large river called Aratsani in Armenian and Murad-su in Turkish. This river is a tributary of the mighty Yeprad [Euphrates]. About 50 miles to the west is Kharpert [Harput in Turkish], 100 miles to the east is Moush and another 50 miles east is Bitlis on Lake Van. Erzeroum is about 150 miles north, and to the south about 75 miles lies Dikranagert [Diyarbakir in Turkish], all larger cities, which had a great many Armenians at the turn of the twentieth century.

Those who lived in the Armenian villages in general were called Palutsees, -tsee being the suffix that indicated where someone was from. To further identify someone, the inhabitants of a specific village were called the "-tsee" of that village. I remember the names of several Armenian villages within a few miles of each other: Khoshmat; Murcho Mirza, where my mother (Sultan Khojabashian) was from; Havav; Nebshi; Goombat; Nerkhi; Sakrat; and Segham, which was one of the smaller ones, with about 700 people. I was a Seghamtsee.

The town of Palu is built on the site of an ancient fortified settlement rising along a hillside overlooking the Aratsani.

An Orphan's Tale

On a rocky prominence above the town, the ruined battlements of old forts flanked the city on two sides. The Armenian inhabitants called one of these ruins Saint Mesrob. Palu was not considered a very important city from the Ottoman government's point of view, but it was the administrative center of a large county [sanjak in Turkish] known by the same name. Before the genocide of 1915 and the subsequent deportation of the remaining Armenians, the population was about twelve thousand, including Armenians, Kurds, and Turks. There were also some Assyrians, Yezidis, and Zazas.

A few miles west of the town the Aratsani River ran through a valley, with plenty of orchards of many kinds of fruit trees along with vineyards on the hilly slopes. There were acres of fertile fields and water was abundant. Large fields of wheat, barley, and goreg [millet], were interspersed with orchards of apricots, plums, peaches, cherries, pears, some apples, and a lot of mostly white but also red mulberries. In addition, grapes and many kinds of vegetables were planted.

My family had fruit orchards, vegetable fields, and two oxen. We made oghi [whiskey] from the white mulberries. Many Turks at that time were fond of oghi, which they called raki, and would buy it from us or barter produce for it. They liked to drink a lot, but they wouldn't make it. We also made lots of red wine from our grapes. For some reason, I liked to munch on azokh [unripe grapes]. We stored the wine in dagar [wooden barrels] made in the village.

There were enough trees around for our use. I remember very tall evergreen trees we called pardi, which may have been poplars. The keran [house beams] were made from them. The houses were usually two stories, with the ground floor housing the animals on an earthen floor and the walls being made of mud bricks. The heat from the animals helped warm the people living on the floor above.

I remember the climate as being moderate; however, the winters were severe with heavy snow covering the hills and fields from November to March. Rains came in the spring and the summer was very hot and dry for three months. Early autumn was beautiful and mild.

Two hamlets were situated near each other at this point in the river valley. One of them was my birthplace, Segham. Built on a flat piece of land between two streams which joined each other just beyond the village and continued for a mile or two to the Aratsani River, Segham had about 60 houses populated entirely by Armenians. Located on the other side of one stream and along the side of a small hill was the second village, Sedilar, slightly larger than ours and inhabited by Turks. There were quite a bit fewer Turkish villages in our area than Armenian ones. The Kurds mostly lived in smaller villages higher up in the hills and mountains.

Each group had its own way of life, customs and language. The Kurds and the Turks did not mix with each other much and the Armenians did not mix socially with either of them. However, as small children the Armenian and Turkish kids occasionally played with each other in the streets of Segham and Sedilar, our villages along the banks of the stream. And on a daily basis the inhabitants of both villages found one reason or another, usually having to do with agriculture, to visit their neighbors' village. So the Turks and the Armenians were familiar with each other. In addition, some Armenians had business and occasional interactions with the Turks and some

An Orphan's Tale

Kurds were hired as workers in the Armenian and Turkish farms. More Kurds than Turks were able to speak Armenian because the two groups worked together more on farms and in winter some of the Kurds lived in the stables of the Armenians.

Segham had a church and a school. We were generally self-sufficient. When we needed supplies and goods we couldn't make, like rice and sugar, we would go to Palu. I remember going there to get a smallpox inoculation. Most of the people were farmers, hardworking and happy, enjoying their lives as Armenians know how to with their way of living. They weren't very rich, but they weren't in abject poverty either; they got along fairly well. Some of them could have become better off if only the government did not levy high and unfair taxes and if the local Turks and Kurds did not harass them. The police (gendarma in Turkish, from the French gendarmes) would collect these taxes and beat you if you did not have the money. In addition, Turks could enter your house, take a woman, or if you didn't do what they wanted, they could take land or occupy it. While this did not happen often, the threat was theirs.

FAMILY LIFE

Although our families had financial and other burdens, as kids we were happy and gay. All day long we would play on the hillsides or beside the stream, but our happiness did not last long. Life was insecure; the ruling Turks would not leave us in peace long. Periodic massacres of Armenians had taken place before World War I. And because for most rural Armenians economic advancement was difficult, if not impossible, many younger Armenian men left the villages and emigrated to larger and safer cities in the Ottoman Empire, like Constantinople,[1] or to far-away places like Europe or America. After my father was born in 1876, my paternal grandfather, Manuel Manuelian, went to Bolis in order to earn a living as a house builder. While there, he became involved in the founding of the Social Democratic Hunchakian Party.[2] Every few years he would return to the village of Segham. After one of those visits, his wife gave birth to a younger son, my Uncle Mgrditch, who was about 15 years younger than his older brother.

My father left our village in the spring of 1907. Years later I was told that I was born about three months before my father left, which is how I figured I was born around mid-January of that year. My documents state my birth date as June 1, 1908, which my father later purposely recorded, thinking that if I were younger, it might make it easier for me to immigrate and follow him. When the snows melted in 1907, Bedros, my father, left his wife, three-month old son, two older daughters, mother and father (who had returned from Stamboul a year or two earlier), a younger brother, along with dozens of relatives, and walked to the Mediterranean port of Mersin, several hundred miles to the southwest. From there he sailed to Alexandria, Egypt, then controlled by the British, where he worked for a year as a carpenter and laborer in order to make enough money to go to America. In the summer of 1908 he sailed from Alexandria to the United States. He was 32 years old.

In 1913 my uncle Mgrditch paid a large sum of gold to local officials so that he could leave the region and not be drafted into the Ottoman army, which had just suffered a defeat in the Balkans. These payments were sometimes called "blood money." With his dobrag [pack] made of cloth, he went off on foot to try to reach the United States. Left in our household were my mother, Sultan; my sister Takouhie, who was about seven or eight years older than I was; my sister Zarouhie, who was between us in age but closer to Takouhie's age; my paternal grandparents, my uncle's wife and her newborn daughter (my uncle had married in 1912). My mother had had two other children after my sisters, but both had died in infancy. A few years after the death of the second one, she went to a monastery to pray for another child; shortly after that trip I was born.

In surrounding houses in the village were several other families of at least 50 other Manuelian uncles, aunts, cousins, and other relatives. After the spring of 1915, when I was eight years old, I saw very few of them. A year earlier Turkey had entered the First World War on the side of Germany and the other Central powers. A year later all hell broke out for the Armenians living in Asia Minor and eastern Turkey far from the war fronts. New war zones were created by the Turkish government against their own citizens.

GENOCIDE[3]

Late 1914 through mid-1915 were heartbreaking times for our village. In the late spring and early summer of 1915 most of the able bodied men from 18 to 50 were forcibly taken away by the gendarma on the pretext of drafting them into a national labor force to help with the war effort nearer the fronts in western Turkey (against the British) or northeastern Turkey (against the Russians). However, no one knew where they were taken, and no one ever saw them again. Women were looking for their husbands, others for fathers or brothers. Some said the government had exiled them from the country, but the truth was that the men were taken in separate groups in different directions, tied by their hands, gunned down in cold blood and dumped into mass graves in the hills, or thrown into the Murad-su. The Turks did not want them near the fronts at all. In any event, none came back home. From my immediate household of about 10 who had stayed in the village only three survived. And from my extended family of aunts, uncles and cousins most were killed or disappeared.

Whatever I am recounting here, whatever happened in our village, happened in a thousand other hamlets, towns, and cities, throughout Turkey, wherever Armenians were living. The fate of almost two million Armenians was the same: their homes and lands were taken, their men and many women and children, slaughtered, while the remainder, from Constantinople on the edge of Europe, east to the Caucasus Mountains, from the Black Sea to the Mediterranean, were driven out and cleansed from their ancestral homes where they had lived for more than two thousand years.

The bulk of the Armenians living in the six eastern Armenian provinces [vilayet in Turkish] who survived the April and May 1915 government sanctioned genocide were driven out mercilessly from the highlands south into the Syrian desert. [Some others in Van province, much farther east than Palu, managed to flee to Persia.] Many on these marches went through unspeakable hardships; they starved, died of exhaustion or illness, were killed or killed themselves, before they reached alien land. Some endured, or were lucky, making it to survival in the Arab lands, which took in the Armenians even though the Arabs were primarily Muslims and still part of the Ottoman Empire.[4]

At the start of summer 1915 our village was attacked early one morning, at sunrise, by the gendarma and a group of well-armed Turks and Kurds. The non-police were called in Turkish "Bashibozugh," or "crazed heads," because of their wild behavior. As I mentioned earlier, there were hardly any able-bodied men left in the village. There only were some old men, women, girls, and children under the age of 12 or 13, maybe a few boys under 17. The women and older children were about to go out to the fields and other parts of the village to perform their daily tasks. We were taken by surprise to see so many Turks and Kurds with guns, swords, axes, and knives. They herded up all they could in the marketplace. They picked some good looking girls and women, some as wives, some as maids or servants. People were confused and did not know what to do, so they did what came natural to them—the women who could gathered up their remaining family members and started to head to the neighboring Turkish village, Sedilar. They hoped that they would be granted sanctuary in the homes of Turks they had known for many years.

The Manuelian clan went to the house of Tar Agha, an influential leader of the Turkish village. However, my grandfather, Manuel Agha, who was almost 60 years old, had earlier decided to go separately to Latif Agha's house. Manuel Agha was a well-known house builder and carpenter who had spent many years as a contractor in Istanbul. He would travel back and forth between the capital and our village in order to practice his trade. He finally had returned to his village just before his second son, my uncle, left for America. Upon his return, he had rebuilt Latif Agha's house. When the government had started a month or so before to gather all the men, Latif Agha had secretly hid my grandfather in his house while we still stayed in our village. Both Tar Agha and Latif Agha were heads of prominent families in Sedilar, as Manuel Agha was in Segham. We knew about each other's families. But as I said, we went to Tar Agha's.

One day, shortly after we had fled to Tar Agha's house, my grandfather came there from Latif Agha's house and told us that he was going to the city to bring us candy and sugar. (After so many years I am still waiting for those treats.) He kissed us goodbye. Those were his last words to us; we never saw him again and no one knew what happened to him. Probably he was killed and thrown into the Murat-su, like many other men. The word went around that the government officials found out where my grandfather was hiding and forced Latif

Agha to give him up. Latif Agha took in a lot of Armenians to save them. In the end, some, like my grandfather, were taken from his house and others escaped, to who knows where.[5]

About two weeks later the village crier announced that everything was all right, that everyone could go to his own village and home. So we left Tar Agha's house in Sedilar and went back to our home in Segham. We were not surprised to see nothing left in our house. The entire village was looted and vandalized. Bedding, carpets, foodstuffs, pots and pans, everything you could think of, was carried away, and the livestock was driven away. Every house in the village had the corners of its foundation walls dug out by the Turks because they hoped to find valuables or money hidden away.

The first thought of the returning villagers was naturally food. Luckily, all these terrible events had taken place in the summer and most of the crops had been left in the fields. They were almost ripe and ready to be picked, but who would dare to go to the fields, on the edge of the village, at times like this? Some brave women banded together to go to the fields where they harvested some wheat, barley, goreg and vegetables so as not to starve. We had roofs over our heads, but we could not live in our homes because we feared further attacks. So we grouped a few families together and we all lived in certain houses, which we thought were safer and in better shape.

At times like this no one knew how many days or weeks were going by. One morning, the gendarma went from house to house, ordering everyone to take whatever belongings they could carry and go to the village marketplace. There they were driven on foot to unknown places, to starvation, to extinction. All the remaining women, children and old people of

An Orphan's Tale

the village, including my mother and sisters, went. My sisters and mother left me to go to Palu. Before they left, my mother told me to lie down next to my paternal grandmother, Arzoun, who was ill and in bed. The gendarma must have figured she was too sick and near death and did not notice a little boy lying on the other side of a sick old woman. Those were the last words I heard from my mother. I never heard about her from then on.

When I woke up the next day, I called my grandmother's name, "Agoun, Agoun," (which was the kid's nickname I had for her) but I did not get any answer. Maybe she had died in the night? I suppose from fear of death I left her in bed and ran outside to go to the schoolhouse. As I reached the main village street, I met my sister Takouhie who had not yet left for Palu. She told me what had happened the day before in the marketplace. Many children, young girls, and young women were taken in by Turks and Kurds, as servants, wives, or slaves.[6] The rest were taken out of the village to God knows where and were never seen again. Many were added to the forced marches to the Arab south.

I told my sister that Grandma was no more because she did not talk to me. My sister brought me to the Turkish house in Palu where she was being taken, but they did not want to keep me. Takhouhie, then, advised me to go back to the Turkish village of Sedilar, with anyone who was going that way, and to return to Tar Agha's house. Since Tar Agha knew the Manuelian family well, and we had stayed there before, it might be likely that he would keep me with his family.

In the late afternoon of the same day, we saw a Turk walking out of Palu with my cousins Vartan Manuelian and his sister Perooz. My sister told me to follow them, but that she could not go with me because she had to stay with the Turkish family in Palu. So I started to run after them, calling them by their names. They seemed to hear me, but they paid no attention. I think they were afraid to acknowledge me. Finally, the Turkish man heard me and stopped to see what I wanted. I was dead tired because I was sick at this time. When the Turk heard that I wanted to go to Tar Agha's house, he took me along and when we reached the village he showed me the street and pointed out Tar Agha's house.

LIVING WITH THE TURKS
—AT TAR AGHA'S

I entered Tar Agha's house and became one of his household members. Tar Agha was well-off and had known all the Manuelians for all his life, since our family also was relatively well-off in the neighboring village. He was a very kind man and very good to me. In fact, he even bought something for me to wear, though I was always barefoot. Tar Agha's family consisted of himself, his wife, his sister called Bibie, a married daughter, and two sons, named Davrish and Pasha. There were also his dead brother's two children, Mustafa and a girl whose name I don't remember.

I was not in touch with my relatives and I didn't know what had happened to my mother, my sisters, and all the other people from our village. Soon I even forgot to speak my own tongue and learned how to speak Turkish better. My job as a child of eight was to be a shepherd. Every morning at sunrise I took several sheep, a few goats, two cows, one donkey and a water buffalo out to the pasture and returned with them just before sunset. As a shepherd I lived in the stable with the animals and I was with them for about four years. Yes, I was taken in by Tar Agha's family, but I was a gavour,[7] half-starved much of the time, in rags all of the time, cold in the winter, hot in the summer, a suffering, weak and sick urchin no one really cared for.[8]

However, in the winter of 1916 when I was nine years old my older sister Takouhie, who as I said had been taken in by a Turkish family in Palu, came to see me in Sedilar at Tar-Agha's house. It was a very cold winter. She stayed with me for a few days and told me that she had lost track of our relatives and friends, and even our sister Zarouhie; they were all dispersed, who knows where? She had been told by the household where she stayed and worked in Palu city that they did not need her services anymore, so she had decided to go to Kharpert where there was an orphanage run by American missionaries that took in Armenian children. I wanted my sister to stay with me, at least until spring, so that she would be safe from the winter's cold, but she refused. She wanted to go to the orphanage and said that as soon as she was settled there she would come back to get me, too. Alas, that did not happen. Sometime later I heard she had died from the cold by the side of the path on her walk to Kharpert. She was about 16 years old. I never heard what happened to Zarouhie, my other sister, or my mother.

About a year or two after my arrival, misfortune hit Tar Agha's family. First, a few of his animals were killed by accident. Then his wife passed away, and not long, after he died, too. We lost trace of the older married daughter and cousin Mustafa and his sister left us, too. Bibie Khanum, Davrish, Pasha and I were the only ones left in that big house, which by the way, my grandfather had built as he had built Latif Agha's house. It was terrible times for everyone. As before, my job was to take care of the animals. There was also a horse, but it was not my job to take care of that large animal. In the summers I grazed the animals in the pastures and meadows, and in the winters I took care of them in the stable. This went on for my years there.

After his father's death, Davrish became the head of the household. As a man, he was the opposite of his father; he was a devil who often beat me severely for no reason at all and, unlike his father, treated me like a slave. I went hungry for many days, especially in winter. I believe there was a famine throughout the region during that time, around 1917-1920. But the summers were much better; I could eat fruit, vegetables and herbs, which were plentiful in the fields and gardens. Because of World War I, no imports of any kind were available. Farm produce, except for what you could grow in your gardens, and manufactured products were almost non-existent. Virtually all economic production was at a standstill, in part because most of the tradesmen or businessmen and their helpers were Armenians and most of these were either killed or deported. In other words, the Turks did away with a large part of the productive labor force. In this way, they cut their throats, too.

In Sedilar life went on as usual. There might have been some other Armenians from my village or from neighboring villages, but I had almost no connection with them. In our village of Segham most of the houses were torn down and leveled to the ground. A few were still standing intact, including ours because it was the biggest in the village, with glass windows that no other house had. My grandfather had rebuilt our house after he had come back from Stamboul around 1912 just before his younger son had left for America. The house was in the center of the village, overlooking the village spring where everyone and their animals would come for their water needs. From the top of the hill above Sedilar where I herded my charges for grazing, I could see our ruined village of Segham. From that high pasture I could imagine that was where I was born, where I had lived with my family a few years before, but I never dared to go near and to take a close look at my own home.

About a year after I had heard of my sister's death on her way to Kharpert, a woman came to see me. She told me that she was my aunt Takouhie (same as my dead sister's name), Uncle Mgrdich's wife. Uncle Mgrdich, my father's younger brother, had escaped the massacres by immigrating to the USA in 1913. I remember it was in the late springtime of about 1917 that she came to see me. She came a second time with a basket full of fruit. I suppose her plan was to gain my confidence and trust. She told me the second time she came that she was going to go to Kharpert with her four year old daughter and a few other women friends and that she had plans to take me with her and put me in the orphanage there.

At that time an American Protestant missionary organization by the name of Near East Relief had taken over the shelter and care of Armenian children who had survived the holocaust of massacre. Unless Turk or Kurd families took them in, there was no one to look after them. We all knew about the orphanage, including my sister who had died trying to reach it. The children were brought to the Kharpert orphanage by friends and relatives, or if they were older walked there by themselves, from faraway places like Erzeroum, Erzingjan, Moush, Keghi, Arapkir, Agn, Palu and many other smaller towns from as far as 150-200 miles away. By 1921, about 15,000 children from two to 16 years old, along with young and old women, had passed through the Near East Relief orphanage at Kharpert.[9]

An Orphan's Tale

By now it was summer of 1917. Late one night after bringing me the second basket of fruit, my Aunt Takouhie came over and called for me. I was sleeping on the rooftop. She told me to get up and go with her without making any noise, because she was afraid that the others in the house might hear and prevent me from leaving. However, stubborn as a mule, I stuck to my spot and did not get up. This put her in a very dangerous situation; if someone in the house had heard her, she might have been shot and killed right then and there. Who was there to protect her? But she managed to leave safely without me. I was not to see her for a very long time.

So I stayed at Tar-Agha's house, with Davrish as the head, and a very mean one at that. I did all of the chores that were expected of me, and more, but I still got a good beating once in a while for no apparent reason. But I remember that one day I lost an animal. I came back home with my small herd after I had grazed the animals on the distant pasture, but I was minus the donkey. That was a terrible day for me. Someone must have jumped on my donkey and ridden away. During that lawless time of war, there were many Turkish army deserters roaming the countryside. We were relatively close to the eastern front with Russia. There were also encampments of refugees who were moving through the area. I didn't see the donkey being taken.

On another day, as usual, I was watching the animals on the pasture on the hill not far from the village when I saw a big man throw his army overcoat over a baby lamb, throw the load over his shoulder, and quickly walk away. I started screaming and hollering, running towards the village. The poor man preferred not to be caught than have kebab that day.

So he put down the lamb, took his coat, and ran off as fast as he could. I was lucky that day.

In Sedilar there was an Armenian girl from my village of Segham, maybe a couple of years older than I. Even though we were together as shepherds most every day, I do not remember her name, nor do I know who she was. She was living with a different Turkish family and she was in charge of a couple of cows. Often we used to go to the pastures to graze our animals together. One evening, about two years after my aunt had tried to get me to leave, she and I met at the village fountain where we had gone to fetch water for our homes. I think this was during the spring. She told me that that same day when she was grazing her cows near our old village of Segham, she had seen my cousin Souren working in a field with Goulaz, another young relative. Souren was about six years older than I was and Goulaz was a year or two older than him. They called this girl over and talked to her for a few minutes. They told her to bring her cows over to this spot again tomorrow and to bring me with her so that they could speak with me. So that evening by the village fountain in Sedilar we decided to drive the animals over to the direction of Segham the next day.

The following day when we arrived, this girl stayed to watch the animals while I waded across the cold waters of the stream to the Segham side where Souren and Goulaz were plowing a field near the village. Souren's father and my father were brothers. They told me that Souren and Altoon, his mother, his young uncle Diran and his mother, Goulaz and Goulaz's sister-in-law, who was a Manuelian girl, and a few others were saved from death and deportation by an influential agha from the city of Palu. As much as I can remember, this influential Turk was called Khamel Agha. He had taken over our house as his summer residence. Souren and the others now worked for him in our old fields, gardens, and vineyards.

Souren asked me to come live with them. I told him I would try to come tomorrow. Then I crossed the stream and went back to where I had left the girl with the animals. By then it was late afternoon, so we started to drive the herd back to Sedilar. We usually got home a little after sundown and then did our household chores.

At this time Davrish was married to a girl from the city, so there were more people in the household. That night I could not go to sleep; I was thinking about what to do. Should I go? Should I stay? The next morning before dawn I got up and left the house. Anywhere would be better than my master's house. I started to walk as fast as I could go, almost running, towards Segham. I was scared stiff. Suppose someone saw me running away? Suppose my Agha found out and came after me? All these thoughts were going around in my mind, but I was running by then. I had to pass a couple of flour mills on the way. Thanks be to God that I wasn't noticed by anyone. Once I crossed the stream and was on the other side, I took a deep breath and slowed down a bit. I thought I was not in much danger at this point.

When I reached my parents' house and entered, Etzi met me on the stairs. Etzi was my grandfather's brother's wife and my cousin Diran's mother. She took me to the inner house and the first thing she did was to give me a hot bath. She took off all my old rags I used as clothes and scrubbed me down. It was the first bath I had had with hot water in the almost four years that I had stayed in Tar-Agha's house in Sedilar. She gave me new clothes. It seems I was feeling good and happy then.

Mardiros Manuelian

By mid-morning I was standing on the second floor balcony watching the activity around the village fountain below. I remember my grandfather having his small table set with oghi and mezzeh [appetizers] every evening on the same balcony and watching the village folk at the fountain before the 1915 massacres.[10] All of a sudden I saw Davrish with a rifle on his shoulder standing by the fountain under the mulberry tree and talking to one of Khamel Agha's sons. Davrish then lifted his head towards the balcony and saw me. He asked me, "Na eechoon katchdan?" (Why did you run away?) I believe I answered, "Na yapajak idem?" (What was there for me to do?) A minute later Etzi grabbed me by the arm and pulled me in, saying, "You never know what that dog is going to do; he might shoot you." For a few minutes Davrish and Khamel Agha's son practiced target shooting. Khamel Agha came out and spoke to them and then finally Davrish left.

For the next three weeks or so I was living in my own home run by someone else, Khamel Agha's family, living under their care and working for them. There was not much for me to do; I just carried lunch to the field workers and watched them work.

FLIGHT TO KHARPERT

One day, several weeks after I arrived back in Segham, Souren Manuelian, Goulaz Goulazian and I left our few kinfolks behind in the village. Etzi had given me the names and addresses of my relatives in America. Kharpert, a two or three day journey by foot, was our destination. It seemed like none of us knew the way, but I think Souren and Goulaz had an idea of the direction. Nevertheless we hired a Turkish guide. We walked the whole morning and by mid-day reached a village by the river. This was the same river that went through Palu and passed close to our villages, the Aratsani. We sat down by a spring and had bread and cheese for lunch, our first meal from our house. There was a wooden bridge across the river near that point, partly demolished during the war years. We walked halfway across the bridge. At the broken part there were two men who would carry anyone on their back for the rest of the way for a few cents (para in Turkish).

Once on the other side we were facing the highest mountain in this part of Turkey. It was called Mastar Dagh and formed the southwest border of Palu Province, east of the Kharpert territory. The main road went over a pass through Mastar Dagh. The guide told that this road was very dangerous because of bandits and rebels hiding on the mountain. There was also a path along the mountainside running parallel to the river. The Turkish guide told us to take this one and then he left to go back. We walked carefully one behind the other. One slip, or some sort of wrong movement, we would have fallen in the swift flowing river several feet below. The current would have taken us to eternity, that's for sure. Once in a while I saw snakes swishing down towards the river through the brush or a swift moving animal crossing the path. I didn't know anything about my partner's feelings, but these things scared the life out of me.

It took us about two or three hours along this dangerous path until we reached some open fields. In the distance spread out as far as one could see, here and there were groups of houses surrounded by gardens, fields and orchards. These were the fields and villages of Kharpert. The three of us walked for another two or three hours through these open fields, passing many almost abandoned villages, most of them Armenian. We saw very few farmers tilling their fields since virtually all had been killed or deported in 1915-1916.

It was late afternoon. I was very tired and unable to walk any further. My older cousins encouraged me to keep on going for a while longer in order to reach a certain village where we could rest for the night. We knew that after the 1915 holocaust what was left of the 25-30 member Markarian family from Segham—only three women and a few children—for some reason had temporarily settled in this village on the way to Kharpert city. By the time we got to this village, the sun was well down. The Markarians welcomed us with open arms, fed us, and gave us a sleeping place.

An hour after we got to rest, another group of children reached there. The leader of this group was Khorsig, a brave young woman from the Palu village of Nebshi. We later heard that this lady had taken this sort of trip many times, gathering the children of her acquaintances from the Turks and Kurds, and taking them to the Kharpert Near East Relief orphanage. She had a boy and girl of her own and saved many other children by her efforts. I think her surname was Sookiasian. She later managed to get to Providence, Rhode Island.

The next morning all of us were rested and ready to continue our journey. We still had several hours to travel in order to reach the city of Kharpert, situated on top of a high cliff and from three sides looking down on the flat land below.[11] On the east side is the town of Husenig, and on the south and southwest sides spreads the newer city of Mazra, which is larger than Kharpert itself. Mazra was where Euphrates College and all the other missionary buildings were located before 1915. At this time (1918-1919) it had been taken over by Near East Relief, along with a few other remaining buildings, including the Armenian churches.

On the late afternoon of the same day we left the Markarians, we reached Mazra. The city was very dry, with sparse vegetation and there was a shortage of water. We had to climb a big hill to get to where we were headed, our cousin Hrpsimeh's house. Her nickname was Hrpo. She was the wife of Goulaz's brother, Hagop, who had left for America before 1915. She and other female relatives had rented a room in Mazra. They gave us food and a place to spend the night.[12]

Early the next day, Souren, Goulaz, and I went to the office of the Near East Relief in order to get registered and be admitted to the orphanage. However, we had no luck; there were so many children waiting in line. There were crowds of ragged children in bare feet. For the next three days it was the same story. Finally on the fourth day we were able to register and be admitted. They asked me so many questions: what is your name? What is the name of your father and mother? What village are you from? How did you get here? Who brought you in? What relation is that person to you? Where and who are your parents and relatives?—and many more. They wrote all of the answers down.

IN THE KHARPERT ORPHANAGE

In the several days I was at Hrpo's house I was with my cousins, but in the orphanage I was separated from them. My cousins Souren and Goulaz were sent off with the older boys. Since I was younger than they, I was sent me to a shelter where there were my age-group kids. I did not see Souren and Goulaz for a long time and I cried because I felt alone.[13] For the next few weeks I felt very lonesome and miserable with the strange boys and girls. They were all my kind and spoke Armenian, but it seemed kind of strange to me. Before I went to Tar Agha's house in Sedilar I knew very little Turkish, just the phrases we kids used playing in the streets. But after almost four years in Tar Agha's house, I almost had forgotten my native language and it felt somewhat uncomfortable hearing it again. I even thought of running away and going back to Palu; it was a foolish thought. But I endured; that was how it was.

Our group of orphans numbered about 100: 80 boys and girls between the ages of four to twelve or thirteen and 20 older boys and girls from about 14 to 18 years old. In charge of us was an older Armenian woman we called "Mairig" [diminutive for mother]. Her last name was Kaloian and she was from the Armenian town of Agn. Mairig had with her a married daughter with her child, and an unmarried daughter and son. This was our household. We ate at the same tables and enjoyed life pretty harmoniously together. My Armenian language came back fairly quickly during this time. I remember that one Assyrian boy, Salim Iskender, was in our group.¹⁴

About three weeks after my arrival, the orphanage authorities decided to move our group to an old deserted Armenian vank [monastery] a short distance away from the city. The name of this monastery was Khoula-vank, about an hour's walk west of the Kharpert city limits. This vank was named after Khoula, a nearby village. Khoula was almost completely in ruins. A few old women had come back after the 1915 deportation to live in their ruined homes.

One early spring morning in 1919 when the sun was shining brightly, we began our march from Kharpert to Khoula-vank. By mid-morning we had reached the gates of the vank. The doors were huge, thick, and heavy, standing eight to ten feet high, and bolted from behind. There was supposed to be Turk living there as caretaker with an Armenian woman and a child. But the Turk was not in and the woman was afraid to open the gate. An American missionary man had joined Mairig and us on our march to the vank. I forget his name, but he was tall, husky, and had heavy boots. He didn't speak Armenian. He went back and forth a few times hitting the door with his boots until the door swung open.

From that moment on we orphans had the vank for ourselves. It was partly in ruins, but standing around the church along the walls of the enclosed courtyard was a very large two-story building. On the second floor were two large rooms big enough to be called halls and four other medium sized rooms. One of the halls overlooked the roof of the church and the courtyard. There were also two large stables and another smaller building next to the church with one large room on the ground floor and two rooms on the second floor. Around the church was a walled-in courtyard with a natural spring flowing from under the church into a large koor (cistern) made of black marble. The koor was also enclosed and had a roof over it in a corner of the churchyard. Therefore, there was plenty of water running day and night.

Khoula-vank was surrounded by beautiful orchards, with many kinds of fruit trees, vineyards, and a good many vegetable fields. All of these had been the property of the vank. It was much more wonderful here than in our city place. Mairig had all of the children and others do various chores to clean the buildings and grounds. The rooms were washed clean; the dirt on the church floor was carted out and the floor scrubbed. Within a couple of weeks everywhere was nice and clean and made habitable; even some window panes were set in. Soon afterwards, church services started to be performed every Sunday. These were in the Protestant service and the Armenian clergymen who occasionally came had been converted to Protestantism years before. The Turks did not bother us because they were wary of the two Americans with us.

One of the large halls on the second floor of the main building was made into a dining room, but there were no tables and chairs. Plates were set on a flat, wooden board laid on the floor, with about 10 or 12 kids sitting cross-legged on the floor on each side. The other large hall was turned into a girls' dormitory where about 60 girls slept side by side on the floor. This room was also used as a meeting hall and on Sundays as a "Zhoghvaran" [Protestant chapel]. Mairig and one of the older girls or boys used to do a religious service, read the Bible, sing hymns, and pray with their eyes closed. In another large room about 100 boys slept on mattresses on the floor. As I recall, our original group had gotten slightly larger when we moved to Khoula-vank. I think it was getting crowded in Mazra with all the orphans coming in. Now, the large group was divided into three, headed by three mairigs.

Everything was new to me; after all, I had been in this group for two months only. By and by, I got accustomed to all the things going around me. I played all kinds of games, roamed the fields, and climbed the many trees. Life became so comfortable. Summer in particular was very pleasant and enjoyable with a lot of open spaces to run about. It doesn't take very much for children to be happy and contented. I completely forgot about the massacres, deportations, the loss of my parents, sisters and relatives; it seems like I even forgot about Segham and Sedilar.

By the fall of 1919, two of the smaller rooms were converted into classrooms. During the day we had three teachers and started to learn reading, writing and arithmetic. All of the teaching was in Armenian. Before I got to the orphanage I could barely speak Armenian, though I could understand it better. We were short on schools supplies—no pencils, not even a sheet of paper to write on. We did the best we could by sharing everything there was and we mostly learned by heart.

In fall and early winter evenings we amused ourselves by gathering around a fire in the courtyard to listen to stories told by the older boys or to the teachers reading from books. A sad accident happened at one of these evening gatherings during the first fall of our moving to Khoula-vank. A Kurd had been hired by the orphanage authorities to guard the grounds of the vank. One evening as we were gathered around the outdoor fire talking and laughing, the Kurd was also sitting amongst us with his rifle on his lap. All of a sudden the rifle went off and a boy who was sitting across from the Kurd was shot to death. That was a very sad night; for weeks we could not forget this accident. Of course, the Kurd was let go right away and we decided that we did not need a guard. This boy's mother came to Khoula-vank from Mazra and buried her son in a religious service.

After a couple of months everything was normal again; everybody seemed to be happy and contented. The Armenian church leaders in Mazra used to send a deacon every other Sunday for an Armenian Apostolic church service. On alternate weeks we had an Armenian Protestant preacher, a blind man named Mr. Garabed. We even had a couple of weddings. The deacon and Mr. Garabed got married to girls from our orphanage. Life went on very smoothly for a couple of years. There was also another small orphanage nearby run by French Catholic missionaries. We were not miserable; at least we were alive, had something to eat and a place to sleep. The best part of it was we were all of the same kind—young Armenian kids. We were happy urchins who did not know any better, or could not expect anything better under the circumstances. But we missed a lot of things: we missed a carefree youth, we missed education and knowledge, and soon we became teenagers. We stayed at Khoula-vank for almost three years.

In the spring of 1922 rumors got going that the orphanages were going to be moved out of Turkey. By this time, a good many Greek refugees were coming our way, hungry and with bare feet, from the west. They came from Caesarea [Kayseri], and even as far as from Izmir, but mainly from Konya and central Anatolia. They were a little better off than the Armenians of 1915 because they had men folk with their women and children and in some cases herds of their domestic animals were driven along with them for a few hundred miles. Supposedly, they were to take our place. Many of the Armenian orphans saved some of their bread to sell to the Greeks.

Finally the Kemalist government of Turkey ordered us to get out of the country within three months. We were to go to Syria, but to no one knew where. Haleb [Aleppo], Damascus, Beirut were names we had never heard before. The orphans were to be moved first, then the rest of the remaining Armenians were to follow. This was the second deportation within a few years, but it wasn't as bad as the first one; at least there were no massacres.

LEAVING THE KHARPERT ORPHANAGE AND TURKEY

The exodus started at the beginning of May 1922 when I was about 15 years old. One morning we bid goodbye to Khoula-vank. Everything that we had accomplished during the last three years was left behind. We walked all the way back to Mazra where we were put up in a huge khan [caravanserai] for the night. We heard that two groups of 300 each had left before ours. The next group to leave was ours, which had grown to 200 people over the years. And in Mazra more orphans and older Armenians were added to our group so that we now totaled over 200. We were divided into small groups of 15 boys each.

Every week in May and June, a caravan set forth. The Turks wanted us all gone. The following morning a Turkish officer came and started to call our names one by one. The youngest and the weakest, along with our supplies were loaded on the backs of 100 or so mules and some horses. The horses had large boxes hanging on each of their sides with a little kid in each one. As the caravan began slowing moving out of Mazra, we said our last goodbyes to Kharpert. With me I still had the addresses of my uncle and father in America. I somehow had managed to keep them safe since leaving Segham. I had also seen my older relative Hripsime (Hrpo), who was a Manuelian who had survived and as I said was living in Kharpert. She had been in touch with my father and uncle in

America and had given me updated information about their whereabouts.

The caravan route was from Kharpert southwest to Malatya, then south to Urfa, and finally southwest to Jeraboulos, a Syrian border town on the Euphrates River. Traveling usually was started very early in the morning when it was still dark and we stopped about mid-day. But because we started late on the first day we continued until early evening and reached the town of Ezoli, on the Euphrates halfway between Mazra and Malatya. After crossing the river on a low, flat, broken-down wooden bridge, we made camp for the night in an open field. In the center the more than 200 people were herded together with their belongings, surrounded by the bridles and saddles for protection. The mules and horses were tethered in the field to graze overnight.

Well before sunrise the following morning we were all up and ready to go. By mid-afternoon of the second day we reached Malatya. We did not enter the city, but camped at a beautiful site on the outskirts. The caravan leader, a Turk, was very experienced and knew the best places to stop. The camp was at the base of a rocky hill from beneath which ice cold water gushed out from a big spring. The water was clean and there was a lot of it. We were told we had to stay at this place for several days in order to bake bread for a couple of hundred people to last for the next week or so that it would take us to reach Urfa, which was still quite a distance away. It seemed like we kids liked this place so much that we did not want to part when the time came to leave.

The next phase of the journey was very dangerous. There were no main roads at all, just mountain paths over passes and down through gorges and valleys and then over passes again. Only the very little kids were on mules; the rest of us walked. Once in a while we had to wade through cold springs, like streams pouring out of rock formations. On the third day after leaving Malatya, we reached an elevated place along the bank of the Euphrates River. There were high mountains on both sides of the swift flowing, wide river. We continued to a flat open area where the river got very wide and camped on the bank. This was where we were to ford the river. The crossing itself took three days for the entire group and 100 or more animals.

There was one large rowing boat that could carry about 20 people with their loads. Once the boat was loaded, it was pulled up the river with ropes and then let go. By the current and by rowing, it got to the other side roughly opposite from where it started out. Another campsite was established on the opposite bank. This was very tedious work, but for us kids a pleasure. While this operation was going on, we were cooling ourselves by swimming in the river, enjoying ourselves as kids know how.

The 100 or more horses and mules were driven into the river to swim across. One mule drowned by getting caught in its reins and bridle as it struggled across. Very unfortunately, one boy was lost by drowning also. Once everybody and everything reached the other side, the owner of the mule was paid six gold pieces in Turkish currency and about the boy, the poor kid was forgotten.

On the second day after the big crossing of the Euphrates, when we were in the Siverek area, the caravan was confronted by a mob of 150 or more tough looking Turks with their guns, knives, and other weapons. It seemed like their intention was to rob and kill us, just as they did in 1915. However, I didn't mention that the American flag was flying at the head of the caravan and there was an American missionary official with us.

When they saw that they could not do their dirty work with us, they tried to play a trick. They faked a telegram that was supposedly from Ankara ordering the caravan to turn and go back to where it came from. Mr. X, the name we gave the missionary leader, was suspicious from the start. He conferred with the caravan leaders, asking them to stay put while he wired Ankara in order to verify if the telegram was genuine. But the caravan drivers decided to travel further towards another town called Basni. They claimed that camping near Siverek meant trouble because the Turks of Siverek were the worst of them all.[15] So that night we camped in a dusty field by the side of a hill near Basni. We took greater care to make our circle in the center of the saddles and equipment more secure. Though it was a dusty site and short of water, we had to stay here for almost a week.

Every day Mr. X went to the office of the Kaimakam [the chief government official of the district], taking with him one of the older boys as his interpreter, to see if the answer to his telegram had arrived from Ankara. After a few days he got the answer to his wire: "Sorry, there's been a misunderstanding. Keep to your present journey." We were all so happy, first just to get going, and second to leave this dusty field. Without any further incidents, we reached Urfa in another two days and were housed in a very nice, clean building belonging to the Near East Relief organization.

An Orphan's Tale

We were glad to be in Urfa. Our first few days were wonderful and everyone seemed happy—after all, we were leaving the terrible Turks behind and were getting out of Turkey once and for all. However, I think we knew that we would probably never have a chance to see our birthplace again.

Although we spent almost two weeks in Urfa, we were not allowed to roam around the city, so we didn't really see it; we just stayed in, and sometimes camped outside, the Near East Relief building. I remember having very tasty bread, circular, about 8-10 inches in diameter and ½ inch thick. Our food was mainly bread and grapes, three times a day. We loved it, at least I did.

After resting and replenishing our supplies, the caravan was ready to continue. The mules and horses were loaded and early one morning in the summer of 1922 we continued our journey. The roads were a little better than the mountainous ones further north and the land got flatter and flatter the further south and west we traveled. Here and there we could see cone-shaped mud huts belonging to the local Arabs. The land was dry and water was very scarce, with no villages in sight like we could see on the northern side of the mountains. On the second day the caravan stopped at a well which the local people called the Well of Abraham. We filled up our tin canteens with Abraham's water.

By the third day after leaving Urfa we reached the Euphrates River again. At this point it formed the border between Turkey and Syria. The river was much wider here than it was further north, but the bridge across it was in ruins. Probably destroyed during the war, it hadn't been rebuilt yet. The French army was in control here, after France got a mandate over Syria in 1918. All of us were so happy for being among soldiers who were friendly. The French soldiers did all sorts of favors for us kids. All of the boys were so crazy from joy that we started to throw away into the river the small objects we had with us, like Turkish fezzes, canteens, belts, anything that had a Turkish label or words on it, anything that reminded us of Turkey. We did not realize that we still had use for these canteens.

The French had tied several large boats together and laid heavy flat lumber boards over their tops, which gave the appearance of a large flat-top. Everyone got right on top of this boat with all their belongings, and there was still room for more. We were pulled across by ropes and within half an hour, this huge craft was on the other side of the river. They let us out by a railroad siding where there were a good many dirty, broken down freight cars standing in the rail yard. This was Jeraboulos. We had crossed the curving Euphrates three times during our journey, which had taken about five or six weeks.

SYRIA AND LEBANON

Soon orders were given for us to board these freight cars for the ride to Aleppo, our next stop. To our surprise, the inside of the cars were dirtier than the outside and there were no windows. We could do nothing but obey the orders. After a light lunch in the rail yard, we boarded these wagons. There was no water, no toilet, or any other sanitary facilities. The doors were tightly closed upon us, 20-25 kids in one car. We could not see outside, but through the cracks in the wooden walls we could see some daylight. The ride to Aleppo lasted all of that afternoon, until the following midnight. During this time we didn't have a drink or a bite to eat.

Finally around midnight we were told that we had arrived in Aleppo. The ladies of the Armenian Church Society of Aleppo had prepared bulgar pilaf for us incoming orphans, but the time was so late and we had to leave at once. In this situation they could not feed us properly. They asked us to walk up one by one and open our hands so that they could put some pilaf into our cupped palms. We ate it like dogs.

Almost as soon as we finished, we were ordered to board the wagons on the opposite side of the tracks. These cars weren't as bad as the first ones. There were windows and pretty good seats. On the following morning we got something to eat and drink. All in all, we had a fair ride on this train, although it was very slow. Wood was used as fuel. It took a day and a night to get to Beirut, our next stop. We did not mind because it was more comfortable than what we had been used to.

In the early morning of the second day the train stopped in a station. We all jumped off and spread out all around the station. We were told this was Beirut and that we had to march to another place where we were to be housed in tents. We started walking. The streets were paved and clean. We had never seen anything like this before. After about five or ten minutes of walking, someone must have decided that where we were going was too long a journey to walk, so we were ordered to turn back to the railroad station and board another train. We were saved from another long walk.

Antelias, where we were headed, turned out to be quite a distance from Beirut.[16] When the train stopped, we got out in a wooded area near a large body of water, the Mediterranean Sea. There were a couple of huts here and there with a few tents around them. As soon as we got off the train, we were herded over the railroad tracks and taken to the sea for a swim or a bath or maybe both. This was the first time we had seen a sea and many of us, including myself, tried to drink the water not knowing it was salty. In Antelias we slept under tents and ate in the open air of summer. Our food was olives, bread, and cocoa for the two weeks that we spent there in Lebanon.

TO CONSTANTINOPLE BY SEA

In the years since the 1915 genocide, many Armenians had arrived in Aleppo and Beirut. The last big arrivals in groups were from the Near East Relief and other orphanages up to about 1923. Rumors were going around that we were about to be shipped off to Constantinople; we didn't know the true facts. At the beginning of the third week in Antelias, in early September, we boarded a lopsided Egyptian steamship which had just dumped its cargo of coal in Beirut. During those days, coal wasn't carried in containers; it was just piled up on every deck and in every corner of the steamer. We found this out as soon as we were aboard. Everywhere one looked there was coal dust. We were soon black from top to bottom. Well, this is the orphan's fate.

Fifteen hundred of us, almost equally divided between the sexes, were on board. The girls were quartered in the rear end of the ship and the boys in the front. The next six days were terrible days for all of us. We were short of food; there was very little water; coal dust was all about us; everyone was dirty and as black as could be. But at least the decks were cool.

For water in the boys' quarters, a huge pot was put underneath a water faucet. We boys formed a line and walked past this pot, dipping our cups into it to take as much water as our cups could hold. God forbid if someone gulped up some water and tried to get another cup. The whip would fall on your back.

A big Englishman stood by the pot with a large whip in his hand. Some boys put their cups under the leaking part of the machinery to collect water drop by drop, to cool it, and drink it if possible. But you had to stand by your cup so no one would take it.

As for food, we had biscuits, shaped like bagels, but unsalted and very hard. A few boys, including myself, had the idea of tying these round biscuits to the end of a long cord and then dangling them over the deck into the sea water to soften the biscuits and make them saltier and more edible.

On the third day out the ship hit a very heavy storm late in the evening. The ship was shaking like a leaf from side to side. If you were on deck, you could almost touch the sea. However, everybody ran below decks. I wrapped myself tightly in my blanket, crossed my arms like an iron bar, said my prayers, tried to sleep, and let nature take its course. The following morning the sun was shining and the sea was as calm as could be.

By now the ship was very close to shore; to the east we could see land. On the evening of the fourth day high flames were visible from the shore. This was the late summer of 1922. We happened to be passing Izmir [Smyrna]. We were told that the whole city was in flames, that the Turks had set Izmir on fire and that the Greek and Turkish armies were fighting.[17] Later we found out that back in Beirut they had heard that the ship had capsized in the storm and that everyone was lost. Some kids who were unable to get on board in Beirut considered themselves very lucky.

On the sixth day the ship dropped anchor in Stamboul, close to shore. We disembarked into small boats which took us to shore and landed in front of an old military palace of the Turkish government. It was called Kulaley, a very large building with marble floors. Even the paths and walks were marble up to the edge of the dock. They drove us into this nice building like cattle, with only our shirts on our backs. We were dirty, black as Africans, without what little personal belongings we had. Those had been lost or so dirty they had been left on the ship. Some of us did not even have shoes. They sent us to the bathhouse. After we were clean, they gave us each surplus army clothing, a pair of pants and a jacket. Size or style didn't matter; at least we were clean and then they fed us a decent meal.

Within a few days the orphans were divided into several groups and sent to different parts of the city. Our group, I can't remember how many, was sent to Greek Edi-Kule. The Armenians had a place with the same name, but it was full at the time. For over two months we lived in Edi-Kule. It was the lousiest time of my life. The dirt and hunger was almost too much to bear. My mattress of straw was placed on the ground under the corner of a building partly open to the fresh air. We had one blanket for a cover. The autumn months can be very cold in Stamboul.

For breakfast we had tea served in an open saucer. By the time we formed lines to get into the open-air mess hall, the tea was cold. For dinner we had a slice of bread with two olives or two dried figs. Sometimes we had cheese and grapes. For supper we had a bowl of soup. If you stirred the soup with your spoon, you might find a piece of carrot or turnip. This went on during our whole stay. At this time the allies who had won in WWI were in control of Constantinople. We heard that we were supposed to be shipped across the Black Sea to Georgia and then down to Armenia. Later we heard that conditions under the new Bolshevik government were so unsettled and bad in Armenia, with starvation, that it was no place to send anyone, especially orphans.

FROM CONSTANTINOPLE TO GREECE

Finally one cold, snowy morning in early December we got orders to march back to the docks. I do not remember how long we walked to get to the port, where we got on to a lopsided Greek ship. We were just happy we were going somewhere, perhaps to a warmer climate. Our guess was right. Two days later we reached Piraeus, the port of Athens. The ship dumped us by some railroad sidings alongside the pier. It was a kind of shed, with only a roof over the space between the pier and the railroad tracks. There were about two inches of dirt and dust on the cement platform, full of lice crawling all around. To this day I cannot forget the port of Piraeus, its dirt and its millions of lice, both of which got on to us everywhere. We stayed in these awful conditions for a week or two.

I don't remember what we ate, but we suffered from the lack of water. One day we were packed into smaller boats. Who was the leader or where the orders came from, no one really knew. These smaller boats, following each other in a row, went through the Corinth Canal on the way to the island of Corfu (Kerkyra in Greek).

CORFU

We reached Corfu in late December 1922 and were put up in quite a large two-story warehouse one block down a dead end street to the right of the port's only pier. At first, conditions were bad. The food was poor and water was scarce. For breakfast we had tea and dry bread. For lunch we ate two or three olives, dry bread, and a thin broth. Dinner was like lunch, but with no broth. Once a week on Sunday or sometimes Saturday we had rice pilaf with a small piece of meat. There were no fruits or vegetables that I can recall at the beginning. Of course, it was winter. But by and by our lot got better. Behind the warehouse was an abandoned fort with a bathhouse and a machine for cleaning clothes. Once a week in turns we were taken to this laundry and cleaning place. While we were taking a bath, our clothes were put into this cleaning machine. This routine lasted for months. This way we got rid of the lice we had picked up in Piraeus.

Shortly after arrival in Corfu, after things had settled down, I began writing to my uncle Mgrdich in Chicago and my father Bedros in Providence, Rhode Island. The Near East Relief organization had tried to list all the names of the orphans and their relatives and received information from local survivors concerning the addresses of the adults who had managed to escape. Every boy, whoever had any relatives in other parts of the world, did the same thing. Soon we got answers to our letters. I even got a dollar or two in each of the letters I received from America. Once, my father wrote me that, "Your mother kisses your cheeks." This bothered me a lot. I didn't have a mother. She was lost. Anyway, whoever got money started to buy goodies, like crackers, fruit, and baked sweet potatoes which were sold at the front door of the orphanage. Even though we were not permitted to go out of the grounds except in a group under a teacher's supervision, it seems most of us kids were happy and contented. After all, we did not know any better and we had seen worse.

The kids, all boys, were divided into groups of 25-30 and each group had a teacher. Our teacher was a gentleman named Hrachia Kourazian, from Izmir. He was about 30, well-educated, a good teacher, and very strict. He lived in town with his mother. Every morning he marched us to a spot below the main fort overlooking the other side of the harbor, a few minutes away by foot. The order of the morning was to wash up, before breakfast, and come back with a couple of flat sea rocks. Within a few weeks the orphanage yard was piled up with rocks and before long the yard was cobblestoned from end to end. Thus, the yard was clear of dirt and mud during rainy weather.

Mr. Hrachia was a well-groomed disciplinarian. He was also a well-educated and nationalistic minded gentleman. We did not have schoolbooks, so he used to read to us from books he got from here and there and tell us all sorts of stories from Armenian history and culture. We were almost always outdoors, except on rainy days, and there was seldom rain in Corfu. Many mornings he had our lunch packed up for us and made us form lines, two by two, or four by four, and march us like soldiers through the streets of the town. He had taught us songs and as we marched we were singing all kinds of nationalistic songs, in Armenian of course. Eventually the Greek authorities forbade us to sing these songs in the street.

We would walk through the town and everyday go in a different direction—to the farms, the orange orchards, and mostly to the beach close by our orphanage, even though Mr. Hrachia wasn't a good swimmer. We swam in nature's way. There was another beach we preferred over this one because it was nice and sandy. It was around from the fort that overlooked the harbor on the opposite side from where our orphanage was, but we could not swim without bathing suits there because it was a popular spot used by other people.

Aside from keeping our buildings clean, we had some work to do. The orphanage had a sewing room with machines to make and alter clothes. I worked there with many other children for about a year, learning how to sew.

Our dining room was a big hall on the ground floor of the building. There were 50 or so tables made of rough wooden planks nailed to the floor with about 10 boys to each table. But there were no chairs, so we ate standing up. Whether indoor or out, lunch was the best part of the day. Also, mail call was another best thing, once a day.

A terrible incident happened in the summer of 1923. One day we saw warships out on the sea. Someone said it was the Italians, who had had some disputes with the Greeks and that they were going to attack Corfu since it was the closest Greek territory to them. Soon the area near the port was bombarded. A few bombs landed near the abandoned fort where we had our laundry but mostly in and around the working fort, on the other side of the harbor where our favorite sandy beach was. Fortunately, the warehouse where we lived was not hit, but a few boys near the laundry were slightly hurt. We later heard that several Greeks had been killed in the town. The Italians invaded the island with a lot of troops. The few Greek soldiers in barracks by the town all disappeared into the interior of the island before their arrival. Now the Italians were in control of Corfu. Italian flags appeared on the major buildings in the port city. Food supplies became hard to get, but the Italians provided the orphanage with a lot of pasta. So we ate spaghetti day after day until the Italians left. I think by the fall they were gone and Corfu went back to Greek control.

It was sometime in 1923 shortly after the Italian bombardment that Mr. Kourazian called Miss Bird, who was the American missionary in charge and principal of the orphanage school. She lived in an apartment on the ground floor of the warehouse/orphanage. Mr. Kourazian had made arrangements to take a group photograph with Miss Bird sitting in the center. It was a reward for our good behavior and a job well done on the courtyard. I still have this group picture.

As the saying goes, every good thing has to come to an end. Corfu was a pleasant land. In the spring of 1924, several months after the Italian invasion, time came to close up the orphanages. The kids were getting older. If anyone was in touch with his relatives in other parts of the world, if they were able to take care of their kin, and if you had the means to travel, the authorities would supply you with a kind of passport and a visa to where you were going. This passport was called a Nansen Passport, in honor of Mr. Frederick Nansen, the famous Norwegian navigator and diplomat, who became the benefactor of the Armenians and other refugees.

At this time we were told that anyone over 16 years old who could not get an affidavit from his overseas relatives was to be shipped to northern Greece to work as a farmhand for the Greek farmers. Aside from our orphanage, which was called N.E.R. Central, there was another orphanage on Corfu called the N.E.R. Palace. This was a palace built as a vacation house by the German Kaiser some time at the end of the nineteenth century. It was located on the opposite side of the island and had been turned over to the N.E.R. after the First World War.

AFTER THE ORPHANAGE: MACEDONIA AND THRACE

Within a few weeks thousands of young boys were shipped from the Corfu orphanages, and from other orphanages in different parts of southern Greece, to Kavala, a northern Macedonian seaport. I didn't like Kavala, but soon we were sent in small groups to near and far towns and villages, depending on where the authorities deemed farmers needed help. By then I was about 17 years old. After about a week in Kavala, I was put in a group of 14 boys, all about the same age, and loaded on the back of a truck. The truck rolled along bad roads over hilly and mountainous country for about two or three hours and deposited us in front of the railroad station in Drama, a good-sized inland town.

Drama is about 50 miles south of the Bulgarian border in northeastern Greece near Turkey. With our bags on our backs, we boarded a train to go to the next station, which was close to the village where we were supposed to go. A short time later the train let us off at a small station where we put our bags in a horse driven cart on our way to the village of Shemaltos. The owner of the cart did not let us ride in the cart; we had to walk along for about two hours.

We reached Shemaltos on the late afternoon of the same day that we had left Kavala. We were left in front of a church and a school. These two buildings, along with one other, were the only decent buildings in the village. All the other structures were tin huts or broken down shacks, and not many of them at that. This was called the village of Shemaltos. We were supposed to wait for the arrival of an official from Kavala in order to turn us over to the residents of this village, but no one showed up that night. We spent the night in the school yard.

The next day a couple of men came from the city and conferred with the head of the village. All the men who wanted to get helpers were gathered. Things were done in an official way. Fourteen contracts were drawn up and handed to the mayor. The contract said that each of us had to stay in a particular home and do all kinds of work—whatever the head of the household wanted you to do—at any time of the day or night, for the next two years. It was a kind of bonded labor, but we were to be paid 15 drachmas a week for daily expenses and if we lasted as long as two years, we would receive 2,000 drachmas.

But where would the farmers get this kind of money? All they had was a small piece of land and a mule; one or two families had two mules. There wasn't a livable house in the village; only one family had a halfway decent house to live in. All the rest were one large room, made of tin and scrap wood walls and tin roofs. The bedroom, living room, kitchen were all in one room and all the household chores and activities—sleeping, cooking, eating—were done there, with tobacco leaves stored in one corner. Their meals consisted of bread, olives and dried beans. The villagers blamed the Balkan War for this sorry state of affairs. Greece and Bulgaria fought against the Ottoman Turks then and when the Turkish Army withdrew in 1912, the Bulgars occupied this part of the country and thus had an outlet to the Mediterranean Sea for a short while. Then, after the First World War, the Bulgars were forced to withdraw. They destroyed everything before they left and these poor farmers did not have the means to rebuild. And into this poor region of northern Greece the government had re-settled thousands and thousands of Greeks, especially from the Black Sea areas, who were exiled from Turkey in 1922-1923 after the Greek-Turkish war.[18]

One village family picked two of the boys to work for them and the rest of us were divided one to a family. I was chosen by a young couple with a two year old girl; they also had one mule. Every morning the young wife and I used to get up before sunrise, pack the mule, and go to the field to work. Some days we used to take the child with us; other times we left her with a neighbor. Tobacco was the main crop; it was everywhere. No one grew anything else as a cash crop.

The work was hard and the hours went late into the evening. After coming home I used to bring a few pails of water from the village fountain while the wife was busy with housework and cooking. Her husband was working in a tobacco factory in a nearby town, Kopru-koy, where he could get a regular salary.

When the first tobacco leaves were ripe, we picked them one leaf at a time, from the bottom up because the bottom leaves ripened first. We left the tops to ripen later. We would bring a load of leaves home and then string them face to face on a cord 7-8 feet long so that they were hanging down a few inches apart. Then we strung the entire length between two poles set up in a special place in the yard to dry. We had to keep an eye on this hanging tobacco constantly. Every once in a while we had to change the direction of the cords so that the leaves could dry better. And of course we had to be careful of rain. They all had to be carried under a roofed shed at the first drop of rain. Some days when there was no field or tobacco work to do, I drove the mule to the nearby hills in order to cut wood and brush for fuel. It was really all back-breaking work.

We Armenian boys used to get together on Sundays when time was our own to talk things over and to see what was going on with each other during the week. Sometimes we used to go to the next town, Kopru-koy, which was much larger than our village, to enjoy ourselves by buying things from stores. In this way we met other Armenian boys from surrounding towns and villages. I forgot to say that at the end of the first week in Shemaltos two of the boys didn't like the place and the whole set-up, so they left. A few weeks later we heard that they were back in Athens.

In the month of August 1924 I got very sick from hard work and sunstroke. I was laid up in bed for probably two weeks. When I got a little better I decided to leave this place. I told the head of the household, but he did not object. He was a decent man, but why should he have? Come winter, what was he going to do with me? Besides, if I stayed two years, where was he going to get 2,000 drachmas to pay me? The whole household did not have that kind of money. He gave me 15 drachmas for a week's back pay and in late August we said goodbye.

I walked to Kopru-koy, the larger town we used to go sometimes to shop, and met a Greek man who took me to the house he was building on the outskirts of town. He had three vineyards in the surrounding hills and wanted me to stay to help him build his house after the grape harvest was done. But I only promised to stay until the end of the grape har-

An Orphan's Tale

vest, about a month's time. So I worked with him, picking and carrying in loads and loads of grapes. After the harvest was finished, one night I told him I was going to leave. He wasn't pleased, maybe because he liked me and had no son of his own, just a wife and a daughter. But he paid me fairly and the next morning I said goodbye.

I headed for the train station, the same station where we had arrived about three months previously. I had no idea what was going on back in Shemaltos or what was happening to the 11 Armenian boys I had left behind. At the station I met the same man with his horse and cart who had taken us to Shemaltos when we first arrived. He recognized me and we sat down to talk while waiting for the train to come. By 10:00 a.m. the train arrived. I bought a ticket, boarded the train, and was on my way back to Drama.

Nearing the city, the train came to a halt and I jumped off and walked towards the city. I crossed over a low wooden bridge between the tracks and the center of the main business section of the city. I only had 80 drachmas in my pocket. As soon as I got to the central square, I inquired about the location of the Armenian church. I was sure that there must be one because I had heard that there were quite a few Armenians in this city—wherever there are some Armenians, there must be a church.

After a few inquiries I found the church not too far from the center of town and knocked at the door. A middle-aged man opened the door and I entered into a courtyard. Upon my asking him if could see the Der Hayr [priest], I was told that he was not in and would not be for a few days. I next asked if I could leave my belongings in a corner of the churchyard for a day or so. He said that he was only the sexton of the church and he could not to take any responsibilities for me or my belongings without the knowledge of Der Hayr. But he finally said, "In your case I think it will be okay; you seem to be an honest boy." He placed my bag in a corner of one of the rooms and then I left.

I decided to go to the town square of Drama and look around to see if I would meet someone that I knew. I wasn't disappointed. While walking the streets and looking at every store entrance very carefully, I saw Vasken standing in front of a clothing store. Both of us had been in Mr. Hrachia's class. We hadn't seen each other since the day we parted from Corfu. Although we were not very close friends, we were happy to see each other. We sat in a corner of the clothing store on the main square. He told me that his boss was a Jew and that he lived in his boss' house. He did chores around the house and the store and got a few drachmas a week. Vasken recommended that I go over to a taverna on a platform in a grassy spot with a brook running alongside at the other end of town. In the summer it was outside on the platform, but now in the fall the taverna had moved inside. Vasken said that Yervant, one of our Corfu classmates, was working in this taverna. He thought that because a lot of men went there for drinks and a good time conversing and gossiping maybe Yervant could help me find someone who needed help and would hire me.

I did as Vasken suggested and found my way to the taverna late one afternoon. Yervant was glad to see me. He gave me something to eat and tea to drink. We sat and talked for almost an hour. About five o'clock men started coming in. There was a tobacco factory nearby and after closing Vasken had told me that many men stopped by the taverna before going home. Before long there were 20-25 men in that little shack. The place was full of smoke. Men were drinking, smoking and talking about daily matters, or what went on in the factory. They were talking mostly in Greek, sometimes in Turkish. A few hours went by. All this time Yervant was serving them and I was sitting on a stool behind the entrance door.

When the conversation in the taverna was dying down and many men had left for home, one of the remaining ones noticed me sitting on the stool. He asked Yervant who I was and Yervant said that I was a friend from the village and was looking for a place to live. The man turned to me and said in Turkish, "My son, you don't have to look for a place; I am taking you home with me. I have a wife and a son about your age. From now on you are my second son." Yanni was the name of this man and Yango his nickname. He had emigrated here with his family from Izmir after the Turkish-Greek war of 1922. He was one of the lucky Greeks and Armenians who was able to get out of Turkey alive. Yango had another drink or two and we were the last ones to leave at about 9:30 or 10:00 p.m.

In the dark my eyesight was very poor. I could barely follow him on the unpaved and zig zag streets. Finally we reached his living place, at the opposite end of the city. They had only one room for their living quarters in a large house with a big courtyard. Like most of the buildings of this size in Greece and Turkey, the rooms were built around an interior courtyard. Probably this building had once belonged to a Turk. After the Balkan and First World Wars when Turkey was defeated, the Greeks took over this territory of northeastern Macedonia and Thrace. And by the last Greek-Turkish war of 1922-23 over a million Greek refugees and some Armenians had fled to Greece. The Greek government settled them mostly in these lands of the north that the Turks had left. As many as several families, two of them Armenian, were living in this building. Yango introduced me to his wife and son who also welcomed me. There was a wooden couch in one corner of the room that became my bed.

The next morning all three of them went to work in one of the tobacco factories. After they were gone, I went to the Armenian church to get the bag I had left there the day before. The sexton wasn't there, but the Der Hayr was. He opened a locked closet in a room and gave me my bag. He said he had put it there for safekeeping. When I picked up my bag and was ready to leave, the Der Hayr asked where I was going and if I had any money. After a few words of fatherly advice, I went back to my new home and waited for the family to return home.

My chores in the new household were to go to the bakery a couple of blocks away and get two loaves of bread a day, on credit of course; and to get a few buckets of water from the fountain outside of the building. These things I could do in a short time. On weekends Yango would work at his original trade, being a barber. He had a chair in a coffee house in the city and he used to give haircuts and shaves on weekends. He charged half a drachma for a haircut and shave. He took me along to help him, lathering the faces, changing the water in the pan. In between I would sit down and fall asleep.

The rest of the week I roamed the streets. Yango wanted to get me a job in the factory where he worked, but I needed a Greek ID card and, besides, there were no jobs. He said he would send me to school, but to do that I also need an ID card. However, I really didn't want to attend a Greek school. Nevertheless, I went to the Armenian church to see how I could get an ID card. They told me it would take two months, so I had to wait.

Meanwhile, I had gotten acquainted with Mr. Garmeerian, an Armenian man who lived in one of the apartments off the courtyard of our building. He was pretty well-educated, spoke French, and worked at the railway station. He helped me mail the letters I wrote to my father and uncle, both of whom had immigrated to America before the 1915 Massacre. Within four weeks my letters, sent to Mr. Garmeerian's address, were answered. I had a ten-dollar check from my father and a fifteen-dollar check from my uncle. I cashed these checks at the church. I was very happy I had a lot of money, more than 800 drachmas, which was pretty good for a guy who had arrived in town two months before with 80, but I didn't have a good pocket to put it in. So I went out and bought a pair of pants, a jacket, and a few other small items. I spent very freely on sweets, pastry, and candy and was enjoying myself immensely.

One evening in about mid-November 1924, Mr. Garmeerian called me into his apartment. He had called me twice before when he had received letters from America from my father and uncle. This time it was a letter written in French from a French maritime company in Marseille, France. Mr. Garmeerian translated the letter for me. It said that I was to go to a certain address in Athens where their branch office was located. There they would arrange passage for me to Marseille and, in due time, from France to Canada. The fare was paid by my uncle Mgrdich Manuelian who was now living in Canada, where he had managed to bring his wife and daughter.

How was I going to break this news to Yango? For the last two months he thought I had no one in this world. Mr. Garmeerian's idea was to go in with me, with this letter from France in his hand, and tell Yanni that since he (Mr. Garmeerian) was a railroad station worker, a letter had come to him from Marseille looking for this boy Mardiros. It seemed that Yanni listened to every word. Mr. Garmeerian read the letter in French and translated it into Turkish. When he finished, Yanni was very surprised. "How could anything like this possibly happen?" he asked. "Maybe this man in Canada is a faker? By the way, where is Canada? I've heard of Canana [Canaan], but not Canada."

But it worked. Mr. Garmeerian bought me a railroad ticket from Drama to Athens via Salonika. I really don't know how much he paid for my ticket. I spent the next few days in Drama saying goodbye to my friends, a couple I had known from Corfu and a few I had made in Drama. On the last day Yeghia, a boy from the Corfu orphanage, and I bought a box of locoum (Turkish Delight). We sat by the side of the brook near the taverna where Yervant worked. Between the two of us, we finished the whole box. Yeghia was also getting ready to leave; he was going to Egypt where his aunt was living.

BACK TO ATHENS

At 2:00 o'clock the next afternoon Mr. Garmeerian saw me to the train. As the train started to leave, he said goodbye and wished me good luck. In about three hours I arrived at a pretty large and well-organized train station. This was Salonika where I had to make a connection to Athens at 1:00 a.m. With my bag on my shoulder, I started roaming around the station. I saw another boy sitting on his bag waiting and started a conversation with him. His name was Khoren and he happened to also be an Armenian orphan going to Athens. We went to a cafe nearby and had something to eat. We met many boys in the cafe, around the station, roaming the streets. It seemed like this part of Greece was full of Armenian boys. We went back to the station at around midnight to wait for the 1:00 a.m. train.

All that day and until the following midnight we were on the train, wooden wagons and very slow moving. The old train was very crowded, mostly with peasants with their bags getting on and off at every stop. After being on the train for 34 hours the train finally arrived in Piraeus. We went to a nearby coffee house for a snack, waiting for daybreak so that we could go to Athens. There was a short trolley train running between Piraeus and Athens in the morning. While we were in this coffeehouse, we witnessed some drunks fighting, shouting going on, a window breaking, before the police came in and arrested four Greeks.

Right after sunrise we were on the trolley going to Athens. Within half an hour we got off at Independence Square in the center of the city, only a few blocks from the King's Palace where we were going. The Near East Relief headquarters was located in the King's palace. Greece no longer had a king; it had become a republic and Venizelos was the prime minister. We easily found our way to the palace grounds and went inside up a flight of stairs to a door that said office. A young woman behind a desk asked us what we wanted. We told her we were former orphans who had come down from Macedonia and wanted to clear our passage out of Greece. Within ten minutes she found my name in the files indicating that I had been discharged from the orphanage about eight months before. However, she could not find the name of Khoren Markarian, the boy who had joined with me in Salonika. She searched and searched and finally said that his file was either misplaced or that he wasn't one of the orphans. Khoren insisted that he had been in the NER orphanage. Finally she gave us each a pass and told us to go to the Boy's Department and present the passes so that we could be readmitted to the orphanage.

The Near East Relief Athens orphanage was located in a building called by the Greeks "Zappeion." It was an old royal building located at the other end of the park-like grounds from the palace. It was a beautiful building with marble columns, walls, and floors. There were a lot of ancient Greek ruins around this part of Athens. I wondered how anyone could have put up heavy marble columns and blocks, one on top of the other, so high to the skies, when in olden times they did not have any sort of machinery. Well, it wasn't for us to know. The Zappeion, where I stayed for two weeks, was a short walking distance away from one of these famous ruins, the Acropolis. I climbed up the hill several times during my short stay to see the ruins. They were in terrible shape at the end of 1924.

During my first week in Athens, I was called to the office to have my picture taken for a passport. The office also had located the French maritime company that had arranged my passage to Marseille. By the end of 1924, I had my passport, other necessary papers, and my ticket to France, which, as I said, had been purchased by my Uncle Mgrdich who was now living in Montreal, Canada.

On New Year's Day 1925, orphanage officials march 100-150 of us kids to one of the best movie houses on Independence Square to treat us to a movie. I was almost 18. This was the first time in my life that I had seen a real movie. It was a Charles Chaplin movie, with naturally Charlie as the hero. It took place on a steamer. A couple of guys were friendly with a rich old lady and her daughter. These guys happened to be gamblers who stole jewelry and money from the woman and her daughter. Charlie also made friends with the woman and her daughter.

There was a really funny scene in the dining room of the ship during dinnertime. Charlie and the girl were sitting on opposite sides of the table. Because of the movement of the ship, Chaplin's bowl moved in front of the girl who took a spoonful of soup. Then the girl's bowl moved towards Chaplin who took a spoonful, and so on. You could imagine the laughter from us kids. This was a real thing for laughter and we laughed and laughed. When Chaplin found out that a woman and the girl had lost their jewelry and money, he discovered that the gamblers had been the thieves. He gambled with them, won all that was lost, and gave it back to this girl and her mother. They were very happy. So were all us kids on New Year's Day 1925.[19]

ON TO MARSEILLE, FRANCE, BY SEA

On the third day of January 1925 I was called again to the office. Three girls and another boy were also there, all of us Armenians. We were told that everything necessary for our travel was ready. The office gave me eight American dollars which they had held, back when I was in Corfu and getting letters from my uncle and father. We got our bags and were taken to Piraeus to board a French ship which was sailing for Marseille in a few hours. When we got to the steamship office, a clerk gave me 200 French francs forwarded to them by my uncle for my expenses until I got to Marseille. I did not spend one sou on this ship since we got our food and plenty of wine from the ship's kitchen.

But on the fourth morning when the steamer was preparing to drop anchor in Marseille harbor, I found out my wallet was missing with 200 francs and eight American dollars. I had not made any friends on board, nor had I spoken to any strangers on the ship. The only persons I was close to were the Armenian kids. The three girls were seasick and stayed in their cabin from the first day on. But this boy and I were together all of the time. He was the only one who knew I had that much money on me. He even came with me to report the loss to the captain. But the captain said I had reported the loss too late. Since the ship was about to dock, there was nothing he could do about it this late. So I was penniless once more.

Mardiros Manuelian

As soon as we landed, this Armenian boy quickly left us because he was headed to another town outside of Marseille. If these girls had not paid the eight francs head tax, I couldn't have landed in Marseille. The agent of the steamship company took the four of us to a hotel run by an Armenian. All the guests were Armenian transients. The first thing I did was to ask Mr. Bogosian, the manager of the hotel to telegraph my uncle for some money. Mr. Bogosian said, "don't worry; everything will be all right. You can stay in the hotel here with us and when your money comes, you can pay me." In the meantime he arranged for me to have my meals at a nearby Greek restaurant and to pay him when I got my money from Canada.

Within three days the girls left for Canada, their passports and other papers all in order. I got my answer to my telegram ten days later with a ten-dollar note. I paid for ten days lodging and food at the hotel and restaurant. Although I continued to stay in this hotel, I now could eat anywhere I pleased. Almost every day many people, including myself, used to go to the steamship company office to find out how our transfer to Canada was coming along. Some people made it, some did not; mine was quite delayed.

During this time I made some friends and even met my cousin Diran, his wife Sara, and their son Khazar, who had come from Beirut and stopped here on their way to America. But time dragged on and on—two months, three months. Money was short, so I started to look for a job. This was legally impossible because I was in France on a transit visa and I had no right to work. In the third month a friend of mine, Sarkis, who worked in a laundry asked me if I would like to work with him. I told him I wanted to but I had no working papers. He told me not to worry and that he would get me in if I wanted to work. A few days later I went with him to the laundry where I was hired as a laborer to do all kinds of work around the shop. The work was very hard and tiring and the hours were very long.

In the third week of my work at the laundry, Sarkis, who had found me the job, quit. But I kept on working—weeks then months—at 65, 75, 85, finally 95 francs per week. There were several other Armenians working in the laundry, but only one man had the proper working papers. Anytime the gendarmes came to check on our papers, the owner used to take this guy's papers and show them to the officers to prove that all of us working there had the proper documents.

Every once in a while I used to check with the agent at the steamship company to see if my passage had been okayed or if any news had come for me. One day the agent said, "Don't go through all this trouble and bother to come here. I will let you know as soon as your passage is ready." True to his word, one morning in the middle of November 1925 he sent a messenger to the laundry where I was working. The message was to get ready to leave for Paris. That was it. The following night I was on board a train on my way to Paris to get my visa. At the Marseille railroad station the agent gave a few others and me instructions about what to do once we got to Paris and put us on the train. This was on the evening of November 21, 1925. I had been in Marseille for about 10 months.

TO PARIS AND CANADA

The next morning the train arrived in Paris where one of the maritime transport company agents met us and took us to his office. We called these agents "simsars," a Turkish word. They helped immigrants who didn't know much French for a fee. After lunch the agent took us to the Canadian Embassy to get our visas. Two others and I got our visas; two other women were refused and had to go back to Marseille. I was free for that afternoon and evening and the next two days, when I had to go to the Gare St. Lazare to take a train to Cherbourg and then embark on a Canadian Pacific ship to Canada.

That first afternoon in Paris I took a taxi to go see a friend whom I had gotten acquainted with in the hotel where I lived in Marseille. He was a country-man, a young fellow, Khayajan Sarkissian, who was also on his way to Canada to his brother. At this time he was still waiting to go, living with his wife in a Paris hotel owned by the son of the owner of the Marseille hotel. To make a living, he made shirts in his room. My taxi stopped in front of an old building on a narrow street. I asked the concierge, a woman behind a desk, if Mr. Sarkissian lived here. She said, "Yes, but he is not in. His friend Mr. Bogosian and his wife are in apartment 43." I thanked her and started to walk up dark and narrow stairs in the hopes of finding the apartment. Since I also knew the Bogosians from Marseille,

An Orphan's Tale

I thought I could stay with them until Khayajan returned. I hardly could see numbers on the doors it was so dark.

When I got to the fourth floor, I stopped at every door. Then I heard the noise of a sewing machine. I knew they were working in their room. I was right. I knocked on the door where I heard the machine. Mrs. Bogosian opened the door and welcomed me in. She told me to sit down and wait for her husband and Khayajan who were out on business but would be back very soon. Before too long, Bogosian and Sarkissian returned. After greetings and talk about how things were back in Marseille, Khayajan took me out to show me the city of light, beautiful Paris. We saw some sights, including the Eiffel Tower, and about 8:00 p.m. walked into an Armenian restaurant and had a good dinner. At 11:30 we went to his room for the night. We talked and talked almost the whole night. The next day we visited parks and museums and went back to the same restaurant for an early dinner because I had to be at the Gare St. Lazare by 7:30 p.m. to catch my train to Cherbourg.

We took a taxi to the station. In the cab Khayajan told me that he knew a Kghghetsee[20] woman and her teenaged daughter who were taking the same train, and maybe the same steamship to Canada. This woman was on her way to Canada to be married to a man who was going to be her second husband and she was taking her daughter with her. We got to the station about seven and a few minutes later this woman, her daughter, and another man arrived. Khayajan introduced us and soon we got on the train. Khayajan Sarkissian and the other man who had come to see this woman off stood on the platform, waving goodbye, as the train moved slowly out of the station on the evening of November 25, 1925.

I spent the next two days in Cherbourg; I hardly remember what I did or did not do. Probably it was a few hours before sailing when I was walking along the street and stopped in front of a cutlery store. I admired the beautiful articles in the window and then walked in and bought a shiny, four-bladed penknife. In all my life I had wanted to have one like this.

On November 28, 1925 I boarded a Canadian Pacific liner, the Melita, bound for St. John, New Brunswick, Canada.[21] Halifax, Nova Scotia, was their summer port, but since this was November, we headed for St. John. We had a very quiet and comfortable voyage for eight days. There were no other Armenians aboard besides this woman and her daughter, Balig, with whom I spent most of my time. I did not have any friends besides them. Towards the evening of December 6, 1925 the Melita dropped anchor in St. John harbor. The railroad station was next to the port. In the station I parted company with Balig and her mother. They were going to Guelph, Ontario, where her future husband lived. I was heading for Montreal, Quebec. I spent one night in St. John and with the help of a Canadian Pacific agent I bought a ticket to Montreal for the next day.

Founding members of the Social Democratic Hunchakian party. The photograph was probably taken between 1887- 1890 either in Geneva or Constantinople. From left to right they are Roupen Khanazad, Boghos Afrigian, Avedis Nazarpegian, Manuel Manuelian (standing behind woman), Maro Nazarpegian Vartanian, Kevork Gharachian, and Kapriel Gafian. Manuel Manuelian is grandfather of author and great-grandfather of editor. We do not know how he became to be involved with the beginnings of this still extant Armenian political party. (Note: permission to use this photo comes from *Massis Weekly*.)

Mardiros Manuelian, wearing army surplus clothes issued in Constantinople, at Near East Relief Central Orphanage, Corfu, Greece, 1923

Hrachia Kourazian's group at Near East Relief Central Orphanage, Corfu, Greece, 1923. Mrs. Bird, the American missionary director of the orphanage is seated center. Mr. Kourazian, the teacher, is standing in row three, far right. Mardiros Manuelian is fourth from the left, row three. Some boys have head bandages, having been slightly wounded during the Italian bombardment.

Mardiros Manuelian, Marseille, France, 1925

The *S.S. Melita* from a 1925 French postcard

Friends dressed up for a Sunday picnic, Providence, Rhode Island, early 1930s. Mardiros on right, Siragan Arzoomanian on left, unidentified person in between

Mardiros Manuelian and Azniv Ladefian at their
engagement, Providence, Rhode Island, autumn 1935

Wedding party: From left to right: Hagop Goulazian (best man), Hripsimeh Manuelian Goulazian (maid of honor), unidentified flower girl, Paul Ladefian (bride's step-father), bride and groom, Rose Sabonjian (bridesmaid), John Ladefian (usher). Providence, Rhode Island, February 23, 1936

Mardiros and Azniv in Van Cortland Park, Bronx, New York, summer 1936

Mardiros outside his shop, Stadium Tailors, on the left, at 503 West 135th Street, Manhattan, New York City, mid-1960s

CANADA

When the train finally stopped at Montreal's Windsor Station, I had no idea what to do or where to go because the only address I had was in Ste. Adele. I knew that my uncle Mgrditch and his family were living on a farm in the French Canadian village of Ste. Adele, in the Laurentian Mountains, a couple of hours north of Montreal. He knew of the date of my arrival, so he and his wife Takouhie (her nickname was Hachoog) were to come down to Montreal in order to meet me. This was the same Aunt Takouhie whom I had refused to go with years ago when she came to rescue me from Tar Agha's house in Sedilar.

My head up, I walked along with the crowd leaving the train and going towards the exit gate. As soon as I passed through the gate, I heard my name being called, "Mardiros, Mardiros." When I turned toward my name, someone threw his arms around my neck and kissed me. This must be my uncle I thought, but I didn't even dare to ask. My uncle later told me that he was just calling out my name to see who would respond to it. He and his wife were staying at an apartment in downtown Montreal belonging to the Diradourians, friends and countrymen. Living in a five-room apartment on St. Urban Street south of Ste. Catherine Street, near the main street of St. Laurence Avenue, were the elder Mr. Diradourian, a man of about 60 we called Vartan-Amou, his two sons Vahan and Peter, his brother Art-Apar (Haroutiun), Art-Apar's wife and their son Charles. Of course, I had no knowledge of all of this yet.

Outside in Victoria Square we got into a cab and headed for the Diradourian's apartment on St. Urban Street. When she saw me, my Aunt Hachoog and all the Diradourian's hugged and kissed me and welcomed me. This was the first time I had been hugged and kissed for over 10 years. In those days bringing an orphan Armenian from the old country to these shores meant a big thing; it meant a soul had been saved from the Turkish massacres, from the misery and hardship of the old world. Late in the same evening some other Armenians, country-men and a distant cousin, came to see me and inquired about the relatives and kinfolk back in France or Greece. Unfortunately, I did not know very many. In the hustle and bustle, the evening went so fast without any of us going to sleep.

The next morning, December 8, 1925, Montreal was covered with snow. My Uncle, Aunt, and I took a train to go 50 miles north to Ste. Adele. It took less than two hours. The train stopped at Mont Royal station for Ste. Adele. We piled onto a horse driven sleigh for the last leg of my journey, which lasted only 15 minutes. Another distant uncle, his wife, and my teenaged cousin Tourig, welcomed us at the door.

The house was quite a large one divided into two parts. On one side were living my Uncle Mgrditch, his wife Hachoog, their older daughter Tourig and their infant daughter Sirvart, my Aunt's first Canadian born child, who was born in August 1925. Also living with them was the distant relative whom I mentioned earlier. We called him Amuja but his name was

Hovsep Manuelian, and he was a little older than Mgrditch. In addition there was Amuja's wife Anna (who was Arsen's sister from Segham), and their Canadian born three-month old daughter, Nevart.[22] On the other side of the house lived Dikran Kharibian, his wife, a child, and a couple of brother-in-laws.

During the 1920's according to Canadian immigration regulations, if you bought land and became a farmer, you were allowed to bring your family members from the old country. So my Uncle Mgrditch and Dikran Kharibian, both of whom who had been living in Chicago, combined their financial resources and bought an 80-acre farm in Ste. Adele in order to bring over their families and relatives who had to stay behind after they left. Uncle Mgrditch's wife and older daughter had arrived a couple of years before. I was the last arrival of the Manuelian family. Mrs. Kharibian's mother, sister, and another brother came to join the Kharibian's about a year later.

During January 1926 my father came from Providence, Rhode Island, to see us. I had never seen him since he had left when I was an infant. He only stayed a week. When he left, my uncle sent me to a French Protestant boarding school, La Institute Evangelique de la Pointe aux Trombes, at the eastern end of Montreal city, on the Ontario Street East car line. The classes were mostly in French and some in English. My uncle chose to send me to this school because the young Diradourian boys, the cousins Peter and Charles, were studying there. Although I could not mix well with my classmates because of language difficulties, after school hours I was happy because I could spend time with Peter and Charles.

Toward the end of May 1926 when the school closed for the summer holidays, I went back to Ste. Adele and worked on the farm. There wasn't very much one could do; there were long months of winter and barely three months of summer. At the end of May the ground was still frozen. By the time we planted some crops, in the cool weather and short growing season we did not accomplish very much. However, we did manage to grow some crops like radishes, lettuce, onions, and even tomatoes. By the middle of September the frost would kill everything. It was colder here than in Armenia.

Somehow we got along. We also kept a cow, and we sold three quarts of milk a day along with some butter. Tourig and I went from house to house to sell what we had to the village folk and to some vacationers from Montreal. We would walk along the streets of the village, knock on doors, and say, "Besoin quelquechose, madam?" In the summer months we kept our cow, along with 25-30 other cows belonging to the villagers, on our own pasture. During winter months the cows were kept in Mr. Aumond's barn. He was the village butcher.

On the first of October 1926 I went back to school at Pointe aux Trombes, but it wasn't what it used to be because the Diradourian boys weren't there. They had quit school and were working as countermen in restaurants in downtown Montreal. I was doing very well at my classes, but I was sort of lonesome. When the Christmas holidays came, I returned home to Ste. Adele and did not go back to school. The United States consulate's immigration office in Montreal had notified me that I could go to the U.S.A. because my father had become a U.S. citizen. This was another reason for not going back to school.

After New Year's 1927, by the time I got my proper papers together in order to enter the U.S., I got another notice to go to the U.S. Consulate, where they told me in rapid American English, which I couldn't fully understand, that I would not be able to immigrate because I was over 18 years old. Fortunately, an Armenian fellow who happened to be there told me why. It seems they knew better than us. So that winter and summer I worked on our farm and did odd jobs on and off in the village. I helped Mr. Aumond, the butcher, and I sawed blocks of ice from the lake. We stored the blocks in the barn and covered them thickly with straw for use in the summer months. For a few weeks I helped make cement sidewalks in the village.

In September 1927 we gave up the farm, taking what little we had, and moved to Montreal. We rented an apartment on Desiree Street on the eastside of town. My uncle had rented a store on St. Laurence Avenue, between Ontario and Ste. Catherine. We bought a used pressing machine and set ourselves up in the clothes cleaning and pressing business. We also did hat cleaning and shoe shining on the side in a 12 by 20 foot store. Within two months I found myself in full charge of the store because Uncle Mgrditch left for Chicago on personal business. He was still a resident of the United States.

During the next couple of months, my Aunt Takouhie (Hachoog) gave birth to her second child in Canada, also a girl, but unfortunately the child did not live. In the spring of 1928 my uncle returned to Montreal. Around this time I was notified by the U.S. Immigration office that it was now all right for me to immigrate since the U.S. Congress passed a new law allowing foreign born children of naturalized U.S. citizens to immigrate to the U.S. if they were under 21 years old. Can you beat that? The U.S. Congress passed a law especially for me! It was time for me to leave. Shortly afterwards my uncle and his family moved back to Chicago. Even though I had been with my relatives in Canada, for some reason I had no feeling of attraction to the country. I don't know why, but I did not find it interesting. I looked forward to going to the United States.

IN THE UNITED STATES: PROVIDENCE, RHODE ISLAND

In the middle of June 1928, two weeks after my 20th birthday on paper, but in reality about 21, I left Montreal by train for Boston, Massachusetts. I arrived the next morning, June 16, at Boston's South Station and changed trains to go to Providence, Rhode Island. In less than two hours the train stopped at Providence's Union Station. I walked to Exchange Place and took the Douglas Avenue streetcar to 339 Douglas Avenue where my father was living with his second wife, whom he had married in 1923, and began my life with them.

My step-mother's name was Sophia Varjabedian and she was from the Armenian city of Moush. I referred to her by the Turkish word for step-mother, analukh. She had a sister in Providence who had brought her to the U.S. where my father met her. She had three grown children from a previous marriage. Two were married daughters. The younger one, Anahid, was married to Mihran Garabedian of Providence. Garabedian was from Kharpert and was a jeweler. The older daughter was married to Vartan Donabedian of New York City. A son, Hagop Varjabedian, lived with his sister in New York City. Mihran Garabedian owned an old, large sized, open-topped Lincoln car. Very soon after my arrival, he was going to drive to N.Y.C. with his wife, Anahid, and his mother-in-law (my step-mother) to pay a visit to the Donabedian's and Hagop. They lived on Wadsworth Avenue in the Washington Heights section of Manhattan. My step-mother invited me to go along with them. Naturally I was very pleased. After all, I was going to see New York City, the wonder of the world.

On the early morning of June 28, 1928 all of us piled into the old jalopy and set out for New York City. I don't remember how many hours Mihran drove, but we got into New York late in the afternoon. On the following day, June 29th, I went to see my father's uncle, Mihran Manuelian, who was living on 116th street near Eighth Avenue in Manhattan. Mihran was my grandfather's brother. Uncle Mihran had brought his wife Altoun and son Souren to the United States three years previously. This was the same cousin Souren whom I had seen in Sedilar and Segham back in 1919 and with whom I went off to the Kharpert orphanage. I hadn't seen him since we had left Kharpert. I spent the night with my relatives in Manhattan. There were lots of black people, whom I hadn't seen much of before, in Harlem, but also lots of Italians. I was in the city during the Fourth of July and on about July 8th we returned to Providence.

For a couple of months after my return I worked with my father who, like his father, was a self-employed carpenter building homes he had contracted himself. In September I went to night school for a free special class in English for immigrants, but it was not to my liking. I did not feel satisfied with what I was learning. I thought of going to a trade school and soon applied to the Rhode Island Trade School. Within a few weeks I was accepted and I started to learn printing. At that time I had a liking for printing. In a few months I was operating a hand press, setting type, and turning out all sorts of greeting cards. The school's policy was to find part-time jobs for its students. They got me a job in a small printing shop. I

An Orphan's Tale

found the work interesting, but the pay was very low for the kind of work we did.

Around this time I moved out of my father's house. One reason I left was I heard Sophia say to my father, "He eats all of the best things. I don't know what he does or what use he is." She was referring to me. I was having lunch and as I left the house, I turned back and threw my sandwich at her. So I decided to leave my father's house and go out on my own. I rented a room in a large rooming house. My father wasn't a big talker. He would often get angry. However, he sent someone after me to ask why I had left. I told him why and that I didn't want to return. Upon hearing that, my father didn't say anything.

In the meantime, I had been looking around for another job with a little more pay than what the printing job paid. I soon found one at Woolworth's 10-Cent Store, working 10 hours a day for 10 dollars a week behind the soda and food counter. The hours were long and the work was hard; we had to carry heavy soda boxes a lot. I quit after six weeks. Providence was famous for its compact/costume jewelry shops and I managed to get a job at one of these places. For 25 cents an hour I did all sorts of things around the shop, but I didn't stay here long because after a little misunderstanding, I was fired.

My next job was with Hengico, a costume jewelry manufacturing company at Public and Broad Streets. I became a silver polisher for 35 cents an hour. Within three weeks I was promoted to being an acid mixer for the silver polishers. The factory was pretty large, with about 150-175 employees. An Italian and a Swede were partners. For a while I worked full-time, eight hours a day, and the work wasn't bad. By the following fall, 1929, orders stopped coming in and a good many employees were laid off. Of the workers who were there when I started, only about 35 remained and we didn't have a full-time job. The few dollars a week we got didn't take us very far. And then I was laid off.

About this time someone told me about a Jewish man, Mr. Mayer, who was in the restaurant business. A few Armenians worked for him. They said that he was going to open another restaurant very soon. I thought to myself that no matter how little the pay would be, at least I could have something to eat. During these early years of the Depression, business was going from bad to worse. The restaurant Mr. Mayer opened was the old Rathskeller, right next door to Providence City Hall. I started to work as a busboy and all-round man, and then a short order cook, for 12 hours a day, with one day off every other Sunday. I got 12 dollars a week and free meals. I didn't mind the hard work and long hours. I was happy to be around some Armenian workers.

Before a year was over customers became fewer and fewer every day and business started to go downhill. I figured that Mr. Mayer could not last very long and I had to think of something else. I heard that Sam, another restaurant owner in the same neighborhood, was looking for help. When he found out that I was working for Mr. Mayer, Sam asked me to come to work for him the next day because Sam and Mayer had been business partners a few years back and now were in competition only two short blocks apart. So I started to work for Sam in his Kneetop Cafeteria; it was the spring of 1931, in the depths of the Depression.

An Orphan's Tale

My work conditions were almost the same as those with Mr. Mayer; however, I now worked only 11 hours a day, not 12. I started on the night shift from 8:00 p.m. to 7:00 a.m. After I closed the restaurant door at 1:00 a.m., I mopped the floor, cleaned up, and prepared things for breakfast. The rest of the time I was free, so I used to go to the next door bakery to kill time. At 6:30 a.m., I started to make the morning coffee and then opened for business at 7:00. By then, all the morning help would have arrived. Most of the workers were Armenians, but the two countermen were not. After a while, the boss found another person for the night shift and switched me to the day shift. Time went on and on. Nothing significant happened.

Perhaps that's why while working at these jobs I decided to join the military. It would certainly provide me with security during these hard times and, besides, I looked forward to the adventure. However, when I applied to the Navy, I was turned down because of poor eyesight.

During these two years, my father and I did not visit each other. I had heard that my analukh had gotten extremely fat, and then in late 1931 or early 1932 she died. After her death I went back to my father's house for a few months.

Then on the Fourth of July 1932 an old friend came to see me from New York City. This was Siragan, a Palutsee. Before he moved to New York City a couple of years back, when he ran a grocery store in Providence, we used to be good pals. We talked about a lot of different subjects at a corner table in the place where I worked and he said that things were not as bad in N.Y.C. as they were in Providence. He said, "Why don't you come to New York and try your luck over there? After all, it is a larger city and the Depression is not felt as bad there because there are all sorts of people." I thought this might be a good idea. I wasn't getting along very well with my father and the work in Providence was not rewarding.

For the next two weeks I was thinking about moving to New York. I thought, what did I have to lose, a ten-or twelve-dollar a week job? I would be able to get that kind of job in New York, also. I thought of moving to Chicago where my Uncle Mgrditch lived, but I didn't want to go even though he treated me more like a son than my father did. I wanted to be on my own. So I decided to go to New York City. One day in the second week after my friend Siragan left Providence to go back to New York, I packed up my suitcase and left for N.Y.C., too. Towards the end of July 1932 I was roaming the streets of the city.

NEW YORK CITY

While working in Providence, I had managed to save $300 dollars from my meager wages. In September 1932 I borrowed $100 from Siragan and with the $400 dollars I bought a very small tailor shop from an Armenian man named Mardiros who was ill. The shop was located at 366 West 26th Street near Ninth Avenue in Manhattan. I was now in business for myself. After all, I knew something about tailoring, didn't I? I had worked on sewing machines for almost a year when I was in the orphanage in Corfu and I had worked also for several months with my uncle in Montreal when we opened a tailor shop. I had the experience and the courage to be on my own. At first, it wasn't too much, but I was pleased that it was much better than $10 a week. I was putting in 12 hours a day in this shop. Sometime later, I even hired a part-time helper—and this was in the middle of the Depression, 1932-1933. I slowly built up my business and I could not expect much better at that time.

I had a room on 28th Street near Ninth Avenue above Siragan's grocery store. After working 12 hours a day, I did not have much time for amusement. Some evenings I used to walk up to 42nd Street to look at the crowds and to look in the store windows. On Sundays I usually went to Armenian affairs, sometimes church, sometimes social club gatherings, plays, or picnics in the summer. During the 1930s, train fares were very cheap, so I used to occasionally go out of town. There was a Saturday midnight train that went to Providence and Boston and returned to N.Y.C. by 6:00 a.m. Monday. The round-trip fare was $3.50. This really was wonderful. Several of us Armenian fellows would get together and take the same train for company. All of us had some friends or relatives in Providence. We looked forward to this Saturday night trip, a Sunday visit with relatives and friends or to a picnic depending on the season. Monday early in the morning we would be back at work again. These kinds of activities kept on for a couple of years.

By the spring of 1935 my business was doing well but I wanted to move uptown to a better neighborhood. By walking around, I had found a small tailor shop at 503 West 135th Street in upper Manhattan. It looked wonderful to my eyes. So I sold my 26th Street shop to a friend named Jack Manuel. Jack was an Assyrian from Persia who several years earlier had emigrated to be with his brother in Hartford, Connecticut. However, he didn't like his situation in Hartford, so he left to go to Providence. One day in the early 1930s he came into the Kneetop Cafeteria, where I was working. He was a talkative, friendly guy who made a lot of friends. He told his story and got a job there. We roomed together briefly in Providence and then in New York City, where he'd also moved. Jack decided to legally take my last name (or most of it) to replace his Arabic sounding name. He had worked at various jobs in New York City, and was working in my store when I sold it to him. He wanted his own business, so I sold it to him for $400 and he paid me in $100 dollar installments over two years.

An Orphan's Tale

About a year before I sold the store I had met a woman at Van Cortland Park in the Bronx where many Armenians and other immigrants would go on the weekends, usually Sundays, to play soccer or have picnics. Her name was Nazli and she was a clever Turkish-speaking Armenian from Sis who now lived in Queens. She started to visit me most Mondays, bringing food with her. What does it mean when a woman who meets you in a park brings you a pot of food the next day? But there was a problem: she was married with a couple of kids. Once in a while I would visit her. This went on for a couple of years. She continued to come to visit occasionally even when I moved uptown. I think her husband suspected later that she was my girlfriend.

One day in 1935 when Nazli was with me in my new store on 135th Street, my cousin Hripsimeh (Hrpo) Manuelian, who had married Hagop Goulazian, unexpectedly came to visit, also. Hripsimeh lived in Providence where I had re-met her after she had taken care of me when I arrived in Kharpert in 1919 to enter the orphanage. She was friends with Anna Garabedian, and had come to visit her from Providence. Anna and her husband George, who was a Palutsee, had a grocery store on Broadway about a block and a half away. So Hrpo and Anna walked up to my shop close to Amsterdam Avenue and popped in on me. And there was Nazli. Somehow they found out about her situation and Hrpo decided to fix me up with someone more acceptable.

At one of the summer picnics that we used to take the train up to Providence for, I was introduced to a little girl by the name of Azniv Ladefian. I believe it was in August of 1935 at the Bell Park picnic grounds in North Providence where I met her. She was petite and pretty. The picnic was sponsored by the Social Democratic Hunchakian (S.D.H.) party of Providence. Azniv and I exchanged names and addresses; this was a good excuse for me to go back to Providence for a few more weekends before summer was over. By then we had gotten more closely acquainted and we started to correspond. I was later told that my older cousin Hrpo had met Azniv at the Ladefian's house. Azniv's aunt had married Paul Ladefian and when she immigrated to America, Azniv lived in their household.[23] Hrpo also had seen Azniv at a government office that gave loans to the poor during the late Depression. Azniv had gone there on behalf of her step-father Paul (her 'babalugh', like I had an analugh) and Hrpo was impressed by her. So she made sure we met each other at the picnic.

By Thanksgiving we got engaged in Hrpo's and Hagop's house in Providence. They later became the godparents of our children. The priest was Father Kalchuchian, whom we later called "the thief priest."[24] I paid some more visits around the Christmas and New Year's holidays. Azniv said to me, "You know, Sir, I am a woman who likes to talk a lot, crack jokes, and be with people. If you don't like that, then maybe we shouldn't get married." I replied that that's just what I want.[25] Azniv said she wanted to get married on the Sunday closest to the next St. Vartan's Day. This turned out to be February 23, 1936. I went up to Providence for the wedding, which was held at the Saints Sahag and Mesrob Armenian Church on Jefferson Street. We held a reception party at my father's house.

MARRIED AND LIVING IN NEW YORK

The following day I brought her to New York by train and registered at the Hamilton Place Hotel as Mr. and Mrs. M. Manuelian. I had reserved a suite at this hotel two weeks before the wedding since it was very close to my new place of work at 503 West 135th Street. Most of the people who lived here were Irish. We lived in this residence hotel for almost two months, paying $12 - $15 a week and eating out in restaurants. My wife did not like the idea of eating out so much and wished to have her own apartment so she could do her own cooking. Once when we ate dinner in a restaurant, the bill came out to be almost $12 for the two of us. (It was a very nice restaurant on Broadway, but I forget its name.) She turned to me and said, "It's too much; let's get an apartment so that I can cook." Therefore, about the end of April 1936 we rented a four-room apartment at 504 West 136th Street in Manhattan for $26 a month. This building was just across the street from a Jewish orphanage.[26] Before the year was over we moved to our present building, 505 West 135th Street, right next door to my tailor shop. The rent was $28 a month.

In this tailor shop we both worked very hard and long hours for a good many years, sometimes by ourselves, most of the time with some help on the pressing machine. I was not making very much, but was pleased. During the war years prices went up. To clean and press a pair of trousers cost 29 to

35 cents; a suit cost 59 cents. One year I made about $4,000. But in 1943 I was called up for military service. Now they wanted me whereas a dozen years earlier I had wanted them, but was rejected. Since I had a family and had to figure out what to do with my business, I was given three months to settle my affairs. During this period of time, the U.S. government decided not to draft men who were 35 or older, because by then the war was going in favor of the Allies. Anyway, because I was 35 (36 actually), I was not drafted and I continued working in my tailor shop. We got along comfortably, with lots of hard work at the shop and also at the apartment. For these many years we were blessed with three lovely children: 1938 January 21 Queenie (Takouhie), 1943 January 3 Peter (Bedros), and 1950 June 5 Leo (Levon Manuel).

EDITOR'S END NOTES

1. In this account Istanbul usually is referred to as Constantinople, Stamboul, or Bolis, as was the practice when these events took place. I have left the variants in where they are written. In spoken Western Armenian Constantinople is usually referred to as Bolis, from the Greek word for "city".

2. The Social Democratic Hunchakian party, the first modern Armenian political party, was established in 1887. Manuel Manuelian (Manuel Agha), my paternal great-grandfather, was said to be one of its founding members. (See photograph p. 70.) The word "Hunchak" means "bell" or "clarion" in Armenian. The group's goal was to create an independent Armenia free of Turkish rule.

3. The formal Armenian word for genocide (tseghaspanootiun) was not often used in the past in daily discourse. Those Armenians who experienced that tragic event usually referred to it as the "massacre" (godorads or chart). The colloquial Armenian words have a more visceral impact in that they literally mean butchery, carnage, the breaking into pieces, slaughter. I have sometimes substituted "genocide" for "massacre" when the sense of a historical event is foremost.

END NOTES

4. There is an interesting firman or decree addressed to the Arab leaders and their people from the Hashemite Royal Court written in 1917 concerning the protection of the Armenians. It says in part,

> "In the name of God , The Compassionate, The Merciful....From Al-Husayn Ibn Ali, King of the Arab lands and Sharif of Mecca... greetings and the compassion of God and His blessings....What is requested of you is to protect and take good care of everyone from the ...Armenian community living in your territories and frontiers and among your tribes; to...defend them as you would defend yourselves, your properties and children, and provide everything they might need whether they are settled or moving from place to place, because they are the Protected People of the Muslims....."

Needless to say, this royal decree presents a rather different perspective than that of the Turkish government at the time. In general, the Armenians were accepted in the Arab lands and found a haven there. One reason for this might be that there was a sizable minority of Arab Christians from Syria on down to Lebanon, Jerusalem, Palestine and Egypt. There were no ethnic Turks who were Christians. However, Sharif Husayn's words might also have something to do with the Arab codes of hospitality towards and protection of strangers.

End Notes

5. "Latif" is an Arabic word commonly used as a given name throughout the Islamic world. It has several meanings, but basically it means kind or gentle. A form of it appears as an Armenian surname "Ladifian," which coincidentally was the surname of my mother's stepfather in Providence, Rhode Island.

6. Recently many Turkish citizens are discovering that their grandmothers were Armenian and are showing an interest in their roots. Possibly the Manuelians may have Turkish relatives who are the descendants of Zarouhie, Mardiros's next older sister, who was probably taken in by Turks, and may have survived, unlike her older sister Takouhie. The 2006 novel *The Bastard of Istanbul* by Elif Shafak intriguingly deals with these historical happenings.

7. "Gavour," a derogatory reference to non-Moslems, i.e. Christians, is often written in English as "Giaour." Lord Byron wrote a poetic romance called "The Giaour," which basically means "infidel" and has connotations of being unclean.

8. He mentions that he was weak and sick, or that he could not see well, several times throughout his account. In 2002, just before his death at the age of 95, my father said, "I was weak for my whole life; I can't expect it to get better now." When I responded that he never mentioned anything about this feeling, he replied, "I don't complain, so I never said anything."

End Notes

9. During WWI, at the urging of Ambassador Henry Morgenthau, who had first-hand knowledge of the dire Armenian situation in Turkey, the American Committee for Relief in the Near East was established. In 1919 it was re-named Near East Relief, the second humanitarian organization chartered by the U.S. Congress (the first was the Red Cross). It provided invaluable aid to Armenians, and others, throughout the Middle East, especially after the Armenian genocide, saving well over 100,000 Armenian children. The Protestant missionaries who ran the orphanages, schools, and clinics were primarily Congregationalists and Presbyterians from New England. Their predecessors in the 19th century had established The American University of Beirut, Robert College (Constantinople), and other smaller schools, such as one in Kharpert/Mazra, before they saw the need for orphanages.

10. In this part of the world, men often accompanied their eating of appetizers (mezzeh) with home-made whiskey (oghi). In 1950, as a small child, I recall my paternal grandfather visiting us for a few days, drinking our supply of oghi and polishing off a large crock of home-made pickles as appetizers—or a chaser. I don't remember my father's response to this, but my mother would often bring it up in a "what-would-you-expect" kind of way.

11. The Armenian place name Kharpert, literally means cliff-castle or hill-fort.

End Notes

12. Hagop and Hripsimeh Goulazian became the godparents of the Manuelian children. As kids, we used to refer to them as "Gunk" amongst ourselves because the Armenian word for godfather is "gunkahayr" and godmother "gunkamayr." "Gunk" is a shortened form for baptism or christening.

13. Souren and Goulaz survived and emigrated to the U. S. Souren Manuelian became a notable Armenian writer in the U. S. when there were very few continuing to write literary works in the Armenian language in America. Goulaz Goulazian became a doctor.

14. The Assyrians were, and are, a small Christian minority with their own language and church. The Turks also purged them from their traditional lands. They lived in the Armenian regions of southeast Turkey, northern Syria, Iraq and northwestern Iran. Their numbers in the Middle East have been greatly reduced. William Saroyan in his short story "70,000 Assyrians" touches upon their plight.

15. Interestingly, my mother, Azniv, was born in Siverek.

16. Antelias is about seven miles from Beirut. The Near East Relief organization maintained facilities there. The site shortly afterwards became the seat of the Holy See of Cilicia, an important catholicosate of the Armenian Church.

17. The burning of Smyrna took place in September 1922 when the victorious Turkish army defeated the Greeks who had retreated there. This event effectively ended the Greco-Turkish war. By 1923 the Turkish government

End Notes

had to all intents and purposes achieved its goal of cleansing its territory of its Christians: Armenians, Assyrians, and the Greeks. Many still remained in Istanbul, however, for another 35-40 years until their numbers fell precipitously after the anti-Christian riots of the mid-1950s and the Cyprus crisis of the early 1960s.

18. Over a million Greeks who had lived in Asia Minor for 2,000 years were transferred to Greece. (Some went east to Georgia and the Caucasus.) About half as many Turks went east to Turkey.

19. This is a scene from Chaplin's 1917 silent film, *The Immigrant*.

20. The Armenian word for "city" is "kaghak." An Armenian who lived in and around the ancient city of Dikranagerd was referred to as a "Kaghakatsee," that is, "a person from the city". However, in the dialect of this area the first two vowels are dropped, and the second "k" sound becomes more like a "g", hence "Kghghetsee."

21. The *S/S Melita* was a 520 foot ocean liner built in Scotland and launched in 1917. Until the mid-thirties, it sailed from England and the western European ports to the Canadian Atlantic ports and sometimes to the U.S. ports south to New York City.

22. It is unclear who Arsen was. Presumably a relative from the village.

23. Azniv's aunt, one of her mother's sisters, immigrated to the U.S. with her two-year-old son. She also had a

End Notes

daughter who was lost during the genocide. At U.S. Immigration she stated that she had left behind a daughter. She later married Paul Ladefian and had three more sons. Azniv came to this country as her aunt's lost daughter and was considered a sister by her new and younger brothers.

24. The priest was called a thief because he engaged in some kind of fraudulent activity. We don't know when this occurred, but according to my father there was a ditty about him in the 1930s that went something like: "The priest, a thief went to the market / And in the market he changed his bill, he made it lower". This incident added further fuel to many Armenians' skepticism about the clergy.

25. Over the years, my mother would occasionally bring up what she had said in the presence of my father. Not being a talkative or demonstrative man, he usually responded with a bemused and resigned grin.

26. It is ironic that after spending many years in orphanages my father's first apartment after he gets married is across from an orphanage. This institution was on an expansive plot of land on the west side of Amsterdam Avenue, stretching from 136th to 138th Streets, and west about half-way to Broadway. After WWII it fell into disuse and its buildings stood empty for several years. As a child I remember walking by and gazing at them often. In 1952 New York City bought the land and built a small park and an elementary school, which I attended for the 5th and 6th grades. It still exists as P.S. 192.

About the Editor

After leaving for college, PETER MANUELIAN chose not to return to live in his parents' adopted New World city, New York. Instead, he lived in the Middle East and traveled throughout the regions mentioned in his father's account. For many years, he was a teacher and administrator at colleges and universities both in the U. S. and abroad. Currently he lives in Seattle, Washington, with his wife.

In 2015 Aratsani Press published his bilingual translation of Armenian proverbs, *Seven Bites from a Raisin*.

www.ingramcontent.com/pod-product-compliance
Lightning Source LLC
Chambersburg PA
CBHW051952290426
44110CB00015B/2204